The Primary Object

John Swain

First published in Great Britain by
Pen Press Publishers Ltd
39-41, North Road
Islington
London N7 9DP

ISBN 1-904754-81-3

Printed and bound in the UK

A catalogue record of this book is available from the British Library

Cover design by Jacqueline Abromeit

Contents

SWAIN FAMILY HISTORY

John SWAYNE – Born 8th May 1893, Birkhill, Forfar, died 17th May 1973. Joins Caledonian Railway on 1st December 1906 as a Brakesman, leaves 19th October 1913. Joins Dundee City Police 19th October 1913. Resigns 19th October 1919. Joins Scots Guards, Dundee on 17th September 1914, No 11149. Demobbed 1918 at Caterham Guards Depot. Meets Bessie Eugenie PRICE 1917 (born London 6th December 1897). They marry at Croydon Register Office 7th December 1919. (Bessie died 14th November 1992.)

John SWAYNE – Joins Metropolitan Police 21st April 1919 – Warrant No. 105445, becomes **John SWAIN.**

John Eugene SWAIN – Born 15th August 1920, London.

Kenneth Eric SWAIN – Born 18th November 1925, London.

John SWAIN Snr off sick with fractured skull in London Hospital, September 1926.

John Eugene SWAIN joins the Territorial Army in August 1939, No. 1478572, and is demobbed as an Artificer Sergeant Major, R.E.M.E., March 1946.

Kenneth Eric SWAIN joins the Benbow Sea Cadets, August 1939. Joins the Royal Navy on 17th January 1943, but is discharged due to injuries received in August 1943, then fails Police Medical Examinations.

John Eugene SWAIN joins the Metropolitan Police 3rd June 1946,Warrant number,128754, retires 31st August 1976, as a Detective Superintendent.

John SWAIN Snr retires as the Divisional Detective inspector "A" Division on 4th August. 1946. He joins Ministry of Food as an Enforcement Officer in July 1948, retires May 1958.

John Eugene SWAIN becomes a Security Consultant in debugging work and travels the world. In 1999 decides to fully retire and enjoy his writing, angling, and the family.

Christopher John SWAIN, born 7th July 1948. Joins the_City of London Police Cadets in August 1964. Becomes a Police Constable,1967. Retires 1997. Now employed as a Paramedic Ambulance Driver in Devon.

Samantha BARBER nee SWAIN (daughter of Christopher John Swain). Born 29th October 1968. Joins the Metropolitan Police on 11th September 1995, Warrant No 196417. Discharged due to injury on duty, May 2000.

CHAPTER 1
FIRST THE MYSTERY

John SWAYNE was born at Birkhill, Forfar, on 8th May 1893. He was brought up by his mother, and has no recollection of his father, Jack SWAYNE, who apparently passed away when he was about two years old. He was happy at Birkhill, but just as he was about to commence schooling, his mother decided to move to Dundee, where she had obtained a small flat at 35 Cotton Road. The family as it was then consisted of his mother, an elder sister, Janet, and a young brother, Jim, two years his junior.

John attended school in Dundee, and as far as is known he showed promise in every subject he took on. His real love, however, was for the outside world of the countryside, and it was here that he spent all of his spare time. He was twelve years old when he met Tom Cuttle, the gamekeeper of a nearby estate, and managed to build up a strong friendship with him, by virtue of the fact that he was fit and wanted to assist Tom in his work wherever possible.

After school he would go to Tom's house at a trot. There he learned how to tie and set up snares for rabbits and foxes. He also went with Tom on his patrols, to ensure that poachers were not trespassing on his land. John carried whatever they either shot or snared whilst on these patrols.

Then came the time when Tom Cuttle decided to let him fire his twelve bore shotgun. To Tom's surprise, young John had the makings of becoming a very good shot, and he had no hesitation of allowing him to shoot occasionally whilst they were on patrol.

With his eye to the future, John had no idea just what he would do when he left school, but he felt in his heart that he wanted to work in the country. He mentioned this to Tom Cuttle, who told him that he could not employ him full time. Tom suggested he would be better off seeking a job with a farmer.

John thought deeply about this. He did not want to just become a farm labourer, but what else was there left to do? At school he had learned that there was much unemployment in Dundee at the time, and the only opportunities that seemed to come up were those as a seaman or labourer. Many of his school chums had told him that they would be employed in their family business by their father. No such opportunity was open to John.

On his next visit to Tom Cuttle, he mentioned his problem. Tom told him that he was that day going to see a friend Bob Burns, who had a small farm nearby. Bob had called up his wife, and said that he had a problem that Tom could help him with.

So they both set off together. On arrival they were invited into the farmhouse, where they all sat down in the kitchen. On the table were three glasses, a small jug of water, and a bottle of whisky. Bob Burns poured out a large whisky for himself and one for Tom Cuttle. Then he produced some milk and poured a glassful for young John. The conversation went on about a beast that was killing all of his young ducklings. It seemed that as soon as a hatch of ducklings took to the water, they just disappeared.

"You've got a badger or some mink causing you trouble here," said Tom.

"I doubt it," replied Bob. "My dogs would soon wake me up if we had such interlopers here, you know that."

As they drank their whisky, the conversation went on. Finally Tom said, "Then it has got to be a damned big pike. Here, John, take my gun and have a walk round the lake. If you see a pike, shoot the blighter, they can be a pest."

John got up, took a good draught of milk, picked up the gun, broke it and tucked it under his arm, accepting two cartridges from Tom. As he left the house, he saw Mrs Burns hanging some washing on the line. He went over to her and asked if she had any chicken giblets in the house. She looked rather surprised, and asked what he wanted them for. He explained that Tom Cuttle thought that it was a big pike that was killing all of her ducklings, and has asked him to try and shoot the offender. She laughed, said that she thought that was a good idea, and told him to wait while she went and found something. She returned after a few minutes with an old battered saucepan containing a useful looking mixture of offal, and a piece of cloth which she said he could use to clean his hands with. He thanked her, loaded his shotgun with the two cartridges he had been given, and made his way off round the lake.

There was no movement on the lake that attracted him. Finally he came to an area of water that he felt was 'fishy'. He sat down laid the gun beside him, and watched the water. After about ten minutes, he threw a handful of the saucepan contents into the pond at a useful looking point. He then dried his hands and took up the gun.

After twenty further minutes, there was still no interesting movement. He stood up, took a larger handful from the saucepan, and threw it in a curved arc into the pond. He again cleaned his hands, and took up the gun once more. After about five minutes there was a swirl in the water as a large fish took something from the surface. John fired. There was a big splash, and a lot of blood to be seen on the water.

"You've missed the bugger," said a voice right behind him. It was Bob Burns. Beside him was Tom Cuttle who added, "A pound says he hit the blighter, Bob."

Bob Burns turned and made for a nearby large barn. He came back with a coil of rope and what looked like a metal grappling hook or small four-pronged anchor. He threw it into the pond and drew it out twice, then on the third time he drew it back with a fish secured in it. Sure enough, it was a pike, a very large one that weighed thirty-six pounds when put on the scales. Bob Burns handed over a one pound note to Tom Cuttle, and they made their way back to the farmhouse. Mrs Burns was delighted to hear that the pike was dead and handed John half a dozen eggs, telling him to give them to his mother.

The bottle of whisky on the kitchen table was slowly draining. Then John mentioned to Bob that he would be leaving school in a year, and wanted to know where he would be able to work. Tom had already explained that he could find him quite a few jobs that would keep him in pocket money, though nothing full-time, and Bob Burns now said he could only give John work on a casual basis, because the farm was too small to justify him taking on a worker full-time.

John came away from that meeting highly satisfied with what he had managed to do during the day, particularly with his unusual spot of pike shooting. After bidding his friends goodbye, he trotted off back to Cotton Road with his eggs. His mother welcomed him home and thanked him for taking the trouble to run all the way back home with the eggs. While she was in a receptive frame of mind, he put to her his problem about work when he left school the following year. Her reply was that she thought he had made some form of arrangement to work for Tom Cuttle. John then mentioned that both Tom and Bob Burns could use him on a casual basis, though neither had the means to pay him as a full-time worker.

The talk continued over a cup of tea and a slice of bread and dripping, his favourite snack after a period in the open air. His mother then suggested that he should go out to Old Craigie over the coming weekend and see her brother, Jim Bell. Old Craigie was a farm situated just outside Dundee, and it was a farm John loved to visit, because he and Uncle Jim had always got along so well together.

That weekend, John made his way to Old Craigie, where Uncle Jim was delighted to welcome him on his arrival. John had only visited this farm on a few previous occasions, but had heard so much about it during Uncle Jim's rare visits to Cotton Road on market day. Jim kept a number of cattle, quite a few pigs, and chicken by the score. Additionally, there was a small stream in which he was told there were plenty of trout to be caught.

He took John to his barn and came out with a fine trout rod with a line already attached, and a small landing net. They went to the stream, which was only about twelve feet across, and Jim showed his nephew how he cast his fly. Almost immediately, Jim caught a small trout. It may have been small, but as he explained, they were all about the same size – just right for the pan, and they tasted great.

Noting with disapproval the fly on his line, he took it off and tied on a new one. Then, turning to John he said, "Come on lad, let's try this one out." He then showed John how to cast, and after a few demonstration casts, handed the rod to him and said, "Now let me see what you can do with a rod." The fishing rod was made of cane, and very light. John had no difficulty in getting the fly to drop in the middle of the stream without getting caught up on the way. Then as he watched the fly drift down in the current, he saw a fish take it. He lifted his rod immediately, and had a nice young trout on the hook.

To John's disappointment, they then both returned to the barn. There they sat down on a form by a bench. Uncle Jim proved to be quite a talker. There followed a simple but impressive lecture on casting, striking on a take, and the selection of flies, which is controlled by the weather, the time of day, time of year and the temperature. He told John to always remember that it is a study dependent on many factors that have to be taken into consideration at the time. He continued by explaining that at the particular time when John was there, the Daddy Long Legs fly with a spider-like body was around in large numbers. That was why he had tied on the very scruffy fly that quite obviously impressed the fish, and it worked.

Uncle Jim then proceeded to show John how he tied his flies. He produced a tin box containing hundreds of various interesting looking feathers, and picked out what he required. Then, with the aid of a tiny homemade vice, which he secured in the vice on his bench, he proceeded to tie on selected feathers. On completion, he showed it to John, and said, "What do you think of that?" John did not think very much of it – it looked more like a spider, or a very bedraggled fly that had been swatted.

On seeing the obvious dissatisfaction in John's face, Jim told him that that was the type of fly they had both caught fish with that day. He continued by advising John to make up a very small vice like the one he had used, then to collect various feathers of the colours that would match the flies he'd seen and attempt to tie them on to blank hooks during winter evenings. Also, he should use a little varnish to seal the silk or cotton windings on the hook.

Jim was enjoying this talk as much as John was, and went on to explain that in trout fishing, you first have to sit and watch the stream, river, or loch, to see what fly is prevalent. Then go to your fly box, and attempt to match whatever it seems the fish are taking, or likely to take. It is important, therefore, to first learn to tie a fly. Your first attempts may look terrible, but they still catch fish, like that very scruffy Daddy Long Legs Jim had tied. Fly fishing is such an interesting hobby when there is no other fishing due to the weather or other problems. Certainly those flies you tie yourself will not cost you as much as those you purchase. Then there is that burst of satisfaction when you catch your fish with a fly that you have tied yourself. It is so very much worthwhile!

It was at this point of a most interesting talk that Mrs Bell called them both into the farmhouse. She had prepared a most delicious evening meal, and seated them down at prepared places. She started the conversation by expressing her pleasure that John was interested in catching trout, and asked how long it would be before he left school. He told her that he would be leaving in May the following year, and said that he wanted to work on a farm until he was settled. Jim then said, "You can come and work here, but the work is hard, and I cannot pay you full farm labourers' wages yet."

This sounded very interesting to John, and he said so. "Well," said Jim, "if you think you can do it come here at five tomorrow morning, and let's see if you are strong and willing enough to do farm work. If it interests you, be here at five in the morning, and I will see what you are made of." John nodded, and said, "I will be here Uncle Jim."

John jogged all of the way back to Cotton Road that night, and broke the news to his mother. She was pleased but had to remark that she could not imagine him being able to get up at four in the morning to get to Old Craigie by five. John assured her that he would be there, and made his way off to bed.

He managed to wake up at four o'clock, and was soon up, washed, dressed, and drinking a cup of tea with his cheese sandwich. Then off to Old Craigie at a trot. Uncle Jim was standing by the cow shed when he arrived. "Good lad," he said, "come with me." He then led John to the barn where he had kept the fishing rod and net. There he took down a large shovel and a big bass broom and handed them to him. He then produced a bib and brace overall and told John to put it on over his clothes. Next he produced a pair of thick socks and a pair of wellington boots that were far too large, but he told John to put the socks on then to put the wellingtons on and tuck the overall trousers into the top of the boots. They then walked over to the cow shed.

There Jim took the broom and shovel from John, and said, "I'm going to clean out a small section first to show you what has to be done. Then you can continue until you've cleaned out the whole shed. It has to be done every day, first thing."

John watched while he swept and shovelled the muck into a heap. Then he walked over to John and, indicating a wheelbarrow that was propped up against the wall nearby, said, "When you have a heap like that, put it into that barrow and wheel it over there by that tree. There is a sewage ditch there, tip it in and carry on here until you have finished." He then walked off.

John got on with the task. As he looked round, it seemed quite a massive task that he had taken on. Nevertheless, if this was farm work, it was good enough for him and he was going to do his very best. When he had wheeled out the last load of muck, he looked round for a hose. In the farmyard, he found a standpipe with a tap and a hose rolled up on it. He took it down and measured out the distance from the standpipe to the end of the cowshed, and it was obviously made for the job.

Starting up at the far end of the shed, he took an almost artistic view of his task. He had never done anything like this before, but felt that he could produce a finished job that Uncle Jim would be proud of.

It was half past ten when he finished, and as he was admiring his work, Jim arrived on the scene. "You've done well lad," he said, "This job has to be done every morning, and then at half past ten, Mrs Bell has our breakfast ready. Come on into the farmhouse, you've certainly earned yours!"

So John removed his wellingtons, and sat down to a true farmer's breakfast of a kind he had never seen before, let alone eaten: fried egg, bacon, tomatoes, kidneys, fried bread and mushrooms. What a feast!

After breakfast, Jim walked John over to a haystack. There they each picked up a pitchfork, then at Jim's instruction forked up as much hay as possible and walked off into the cowshed with it. They then proceeded to set out what Jim referred to as 'the bedding for the beasts'. After an hour's work Jim lead the way to a nearby meadow where his cows were resting. He stopped by a five barred gate, and with a stick hammered on the top of it about five times. He then opened the gate. The cows, upon hearing the noises, had started to walk towards the gate. "Walk slowly towards the cowshed," said Jim. "I'll follow behind the last one, and when they are all inside I'll close up the shed." John was surprised to see that each animal had its own stall or byre, and made for it. Then Mrs Bell appeared with two large buckets, and milking began. John's job was to take the full buckets from one of the milkers, and pour the contents into milk churns placed ready.

At four o'clock in the afternoon, John was again invited into the farmhouse. Uncle Jim quizzed him on whether he thought he could do the work, and was most happy when John told him that he liked the opportunity of assisting in the farm work when he left school. He was then told that he could come to the farm as often as he liked to see how the work progressed. Then, if when he left school, he wanted to continue as a farm worker for a while, he would be paid ten shillings a week, with all food provided, and he could sleep in the spare room in the farm house. John told him that he had seen enough, and would definitely start work at Old Craigie when he left school the following year. Jim slapped John on the back and said, "That's the stuff, lad, and here's a pound note, don't spend it all at once. You'll be earning good money when you start here.

John took his time going home that late afternoon. He had worked hard, and felt that he liked the work because it would keep him fit, and he enjoyed the open air life. But he did not want to remain a farm labourer all of his life, and felt that there were far better things to do in life.

Back home he gave the good news to his mother. He offered her the pound note that Uncle Jim had given him, but she would not accept it. Instead she produced a small tin from the kitchen and told him to put the pound note in the tin and keep the tin in a safe place. He could keep all of the cash he obtained for doing odd jobs in that tin, so that when he wanted money for something important he would have the necessary cash available. Furthermore, he would not have to worry, or need to borrow from others. Finally she warned him not to be shy about accepting money for work he had done, in fact to make a point of ensuring that he was paid for his efforts.

John was very tired at this point, and went off to bed early that night. He had a little difficulty in getting to sleep, because the wise words of his mother worried him. He had never asked his friends for payment, as he enjoyed doing odd jobs; but perhaps she was right. He had already been bitten by the fishing bug, and had seen a fly rod in the tackle shop window that he would love. The trouble was that it cost five pounds, and he could never accumulate that sort of money without getting paid for work he did..

He continued with his schooling, and was always amongst those at the top of the class. He kept up his contact with Tom Cuttle and Bob Burns, and occasionally earned a few pence for the odd jobs he did for them. He also received small payments from Tom Cuttle for assisting on a shoot drive on Tom's estate, when he was even given a pheasant as well. This was much to the pleasure of his mother, who treated the pheasant like the legendary Christmas turkey!

In May 1907, John left school, and commenced working for Jim Bell. He thoroughly enjoyed the work, but with branches of his family doing well in business, he cast his eyes further afield than continuing as a farm labourer for the rest of his life.

Then, at a shoot, where he was working as a beater for Tom Cuttle, one of his fellow beaters started talking about his work on the railway, a job that paid him two pounds a week. He had been working for the railway for two years, and said it even had a pension at the end of your service. Furthermore, they were always interested in interviewing new recruits in the service

This all sounded very interesting, so John took down the particulars of the Caledonian Railway Company, and told his friend that he would write to them when he returned home that evening.

John had developed superb handwriting whilst at school, and being an extremely thorough individual, he spent the evening working out what he could say. As for references, he could only give his school, Tom Cuttle, the Keeper who he assisted from time to time, and his Uncle Jim at Old Craigie.

Having submitted his application, John just got on with his work at the farm, first informing his uncle that he had made the application. Jim received the news with mixed feelings. He was sad to hear that John had decided to move on, but admired him for his go-ahead spirit.

Work at the farm carried on as before. After about a month, Jim told his nephew that he had received a request from Caledonian Railways for a reference for him, and that he had sent one in to say that John was a hard worker, honest, and he would be sorry to see him leave.

This was good news. Now he was waiting on tenterhooks for some communication asking him to attend an interview. Time seemed to just drag on, to the extent that the days felt very long. Then, on his return to Cotton Road, from Old Craigie one evening, John found a letter that had arrived during the day, waiting for him. This was from the Caledonian Railway, asking him to attend their Dundee offices for an interview the following day at 9am.

His excitement grew out of all proportion. Then commenced a period of worry. He had never owned a suit of any kind, and he was concerned about how he could present himself in his Sunday best farm clothes.

The following morning, John attended the Caledonian offices. He did not know what to expect, but vowed to present himself well. He was interviewed by the Traffic Superintendent, who, to John's surprise, had even been in touch with his former headmaster, who had given him quite a glowing report

Although the interview did not take long, John felt that he had been standing in front of the Superintendent for ages. Finally the man said to him, "You will start work at Dundee Station at 8am on Monday John, you will be what we refer to as a Brakesman. You will be called on for all manner of general work, but after your work on your uncle's farm, I do not think you will have any difficulty."

John took to this work like the proverbial duck to water. His tasks were many and varied. On arrival at the station at the beginning of his shift, he never knew just what he would be doing, from sweeping up the platforms or walking along miles of track, tapping the lines and ensuring that the rail grips were firm, to manually changing track junctions, and even learning Morse Code for sending short messages to the adjoining stations on a strange sending device on the communication desk.

He also found that he had a new circle of friends, although he still kept in close touch with Tom Cuttle and his Uncle Jim. One of his new friends was Sergeant McKenzie of the Dundee City Police.

As much as he enjoyed the variation of his work on the railway, John still had his eyes on better things. Bob McKenzie, his Police friend, told him that the City Police were still short of local men because those young men preferred to work either on farms, for family businesses, or to travel far afield.

John could not ignore this latest suggestion. He had worked for the railway for nearly six years before he decided to make an application to join the Dundee City Police. He attended an interview, and then was told that he could begin working as a Police Constable on 19th October 1913. He submitted his resignation to Caledonian Railway, who had already given the Police a fine reference for him, and commenced work as a Constable in Dundee.

During those years, John's love of fishing, first brought to the fore at Old Craigie, took care of his spare time. He saved up every penny of spare cash he had, and ultimately purchased the beautiful Greenheart trout rod that he had seen in the Dundee fishing tackle shop, whilst still at school.

He started to fish certain local areas of the River Tay, and although he had purchased his rod for trout fishing, he was soon into salmon fishing as well. He enjoyed the open air and nature very much, and he was always bringing home small salmon and fairly large trout to his mother. Then he found himself enjoying the respect of water bailiffs who allowed him to fish private waters, which produced some wonderful results.

Police Constable John Swayne began work for Dundee City Police on 19th October,1913. He was measured and fitted with a uniform, and fully kitted out. There followed about three days' personal instruction by Sergeant McKenzie, and thereafter he was taken out by the sergeant on beat patrol for one day, then released to patrol on his own.

It was soon very obvious to John that a Policeman was greatly respected by all. This was a point brought home to him when he was on patrol near the docks. As he walked at a measured step towards a group of workers, thinking of stepping into the roadway or waiting for them to part to let him through, they parted as one and he walked through the group.

On another occasion, when he was advised that there was a fight or disturbance in a public house, he walked into the bar and everything went dead quiet. Two characters who were at the centre of the argument were indicated to him, and he just went over to them and told them to leave the bar immediately. They left as requested.

On his return to the station that particular evening, Sergeant McKenzie came over to John and complimented him on the way he had calmly entered the troublesome public house and dealt with the matter. He had heard about it from the publican, who was also complimentary about the calm and official manner in which John had dealt with the incident.

He was enjoying his Police work, and seemed to have gained the full confidence and appreciation of his bosses on his ability to look after his beat, and everything went off well for nearly twelve months, when war broke out between Britain and Germany. Then Sergeant McKenzie told John that he and some of the other officers were going to volunteer for the Scots Guards. Immediately, John told the sergeant that he too would join up with them.

On 17th September 1914, John and his friends, along with his brother Jim, joined the Scots Guards at Dundee. They were soon sent to France, where during the battles that followed some were killed, and John was wounded on three occasions. On the last occasion, 11149 Guardsman John Swayne, his trench blown up in shelling, was buried. He was, however, finally dug out of the morass by his comrades and, found to have a badly crushed chest, he was passed back to the field hospital for treatment, and from there to Caterham, Guards Depot in Surrey. Nothing further was heard of his brother Jim, who was subsequently listed as killed in action.

Whilst at Caterham, on a period of sick leave, John began to study the many subjects he had missed out on during his elementary schooling in Dundee, and earned an Army Third Class Educational certificate.

From Caterham Guards Depot, soldiers on local leave generally made their way to Croydon, the largest town in the area. The routine was to travel from Caterham by bus to Purley, then to take another bus into Croydon. It was at Purley that John met Bessie Eugenie PRICE, who worked at Sainsbury's store, situated at the road junction of the Brighton Road, with Godston Road.

From that casual meeting, a great friendship developed. At the time of the original meeting, Police Constable Jack McPhail was on point duty at this road junction. There was not a lot of traffic at the time, but he had to be there in case there was an accident. Bessie introduced John to Jack McPhail, who was her brother-in-law, and told him that she was living at Kenley with her sister Nettie, and Jack.

Subsequently, John and Bessie met regularly and he also called on her at the cottage where the McPhails lived and became engaged in long conversations with Jack McPhail about the London Metropolitan Police that Jack was serving with. John was surprised to hear how a single Police Force covered such a vast area, and spent much of the time at the cottage discussing policing in London. Jack also told him that the Metropolitan Police were always looking for recruits.

John earned promotion to Drill Sergeant in the Scots Guards, and was subsequently transferred to the Army reserve, on demobilisation on 17th January 1919. Life thereafter continued in a pleasant and happy vein. John applied to join the Metropolitan Police, and, as he and Bessie had become very close in their relationship, they decided to get married.

His application to join the Metropolitan Police was a quite straightforward affair, he thought, but on this point the 'mystery' was solved. Two days after receiving the application the Police authorities sent for him. All very worried, he made his way to Scotland Yard. There he was informed that the registrar at Birkhill who had accepted the registration of his birth had mistakenly recorded his name SWAYNE as SWAIN, therefore it must be accepted as his correct name, and all letters and communications relating to him must thereafter be in the name SWAIN. At long last the mystery was solved.

John's application to join the Metropolitan Police was

confirmed, and he commenced working at Leman Street Police station in the East End of London as a uniformed Police Constable on 21st.April 1919. Later, in December that year, John and Bessie married at Croydon Register office.

CHAPTER 2
THE GOOD LIFE BEGINS

Life now took on a completely new angle. Bessie found a suitable flat in Haydons Road, Wimbledon, and the couple settled down to married life.

Yet, happy though they may have been, John found it difficult living in Wimbledon and having to travel to London to work at the odd hours required by the Police service. He therefore began looking round for a more local home address near his work. He found a suitable flat in Murdle Street, Whitechapel, and they both moved in. Life then became far more pleasant, because John had no worries about getting to work on time.

He soon found that policing the East End of London was a lot different from his old work with the Dundee City Police, but once he had mastered his way round his beats covered by Leman Street Police Station, life took on quite an easy outlook. He had always retained his general feeling of fitness, although he had been worried, even when he went for his medical examination to get into the London Police, after his last shocking experience in France during the war.

It was an incident that occurred after about eighteen months as a beat officer that brought home to him full satisfaction regarding his fitness. Whilst on solitary patrol on night duty just before Christmas 1920, he heard the sound of breaking glass coming from Cannon Street

Road. He quietly walked in the direction of the sound, and noticed some broken glass on the pavement by some shop premises. He stood in a deep doorway and waited. It was half past three in the morning.

Twenty minutes later, he saw a door open and a man walk out carrying a bag of some sort. As the man walked away, John came out of his hiding place and went after him. His quarry immediately started to run, so John cantered after him. He felt he could have caught him quickly, but wanted to wear him out first, as he did not fancy fighting a man who was still fresh, who might even be armed. It was not long, however, before John was led off his home ground. He grabbed the man and found the bag contained some cutlery, a small clock and some loose cash.

John told his prisoner, who was well puffed out, that he would take him to Leman Street Police Station, and marched him off. In truth, John did not know where he was, and just took a direction that his instinct told him was correct. He was lucky he came to Whitechapel high Street, and was soon with his prisoner in the station. There, having charged the man and placed him in a cell, he started listing the property found in the bag. His superiors complimented him on the arrest, but when they asked him for details of where he had actually arrested the prisoner, John could not tell them just where he was at the time. Some time was then spent going over the local maps, only to find that he had arrested the man on Old Street Police Station ground. Not that this really mattered, further than that an arresting policeman must know the name of the street when he gives his evidence in court. In any event, the offence of office breaking had been committed on Leman Street ground.

It was whilst John and Bessie were living in the flat at Murdle Street that I – the author – arrived on the scene in August 1920 to be named and christened John Eugene Swain – John, after my father, and Eugene in respect of my mother's second name, Eugenie. The latter was a name that I tried unsuccessfully not to use – it always seemed to surface ultimately.

Police Constable John Swain continued to produce successful results for his superiors. On another occasion, he recognised a man who was listed as wanted in the Police Gazette. He walked towards him, but the man noticed and immediately took off. John chased him down Leman Street along Cable Street, and deep into dockland. Finally the man stopped, turned and shaped up to John. A fight ensued in which John was able to subdue his opponent. He then began to lead the man back to the station – or so he thought.

"Where do you think you are taking me?" asked his prisoner.

"Leman Street," replied John.

"Bloody funny way to get to Leman Street!" was the man's remark. John realised that he was going in the wrong direction, but was still not sure which way to go. There was only one thing left to do. He held his prisoner up against a wall, and shook him until he pointed him in the right direction.

He arrived, highly relieved, at Leman Street Station with his man, to be congratulated by the Detective Sergeant, who said that he wanted John to leave his uniform at home the next day, and to come out in plain clothes. He said the bosses wanted John to continue his successful run of arresting thieves who, in the locality, seemed to be successful in evading the patrolling uniformed officers. After that day, John never wore a uniform again.

Bessie was pleased to hear that John would now be working in plain clothes, and told him that she thought that this was a sort of promotion. John, however, told her in no uncertain manner that, although it may have shown that his superiors regarded him in a better light, promotion or transfer to the actual Criminal Investigation Department were still a long way off.

On his first day in plain clothes, John reported to the C.I.D. office at Leman Street station at 9am. There he was told that he could now patrol anywhere in the "H" Division area, and advised to thoroughly examine the Divisional area map pinned up in the office. After about a quarter of an hour, the Detective Sergeant came over to him and told him that he did not want him wasting his time poring over the map, but to use every genuine opportunity to ensure that he knew the boundaries and streets by name. He qualified this by advising John to be sure in future that when he arrested people, he did it on his ground, and not in someone else's area, because that caused internal friction between Police divisions, which was bad! This sounded like advice to be heeded, and John decided he would abide by the wisdom of his Sergeant.

John's first self-imposed task was to walk the entire boundary of his division. This took him a lot longer than he had imagined, and he jog-trotted most of the way. He finally returned to the station and asked his Detective Sergeant if there was a particular area that he wanted him to attend to. The Sergeant told him to firstly find a suitable place in Cable Street where he could hide up and watch some of the cafés used by seamen in that area.

This presented no difficulty, and he soon struck up a

friendship with a Jewish poultry dealer, Joe Simons, who had no objection to his using an upstairs room where he kept his cleaning gear. This was an ideal vantage point, from where he could plainly see the entrances of two cafes.

On his third day above Joe Simon's shop, John saw a man go into the nearest café carrying a bag which obviously contained something. The man was white, and looked like a seaman from his clothing. About a half hour later he came out, and walked towards the second cafe. John went downstairs and into the street; he followed the character, and stopped him before he entered the cafe. He asked him what he had in the bag, but all the man would say was, "Is a mina property."

He was obviously a foreigner, probably Italian, and very excitable. John looked inside the bag, there was a model of a ship made in something like marble, and a brass clock of the type he had seen in ships cabins marked Genoa. John told the protesting seaman that he was going to arrest him and take him to Leman Street Police Station. All his prisoner would continue to say was: "Is a mina property."

At the station, John's his C.I.D. Sergeant came out and asked him what he had brought in. John told him what he had seen, and said that he thought the man was trying to sell stolen property. The sergeant did not seem very pleased, and said, "We will need to know a lot more than that." The prisoner was placed in a cell while John and the Sergeant took the property into the C.I.D. office. Meanwhile he had sent for an Officer who spoke Italian.

It turned out that the seaman was from an Italian ship in the pool of London. The model ship was made of marble, and had been made in the ships home port of

Genoa. As to the brass clock, the probability was that it had been stolen from this man's ship.

The next trip was to a ship in the Pool of London. The Captain welcomed John and the Sergeant on board, and when shown the clock, he indicated that it was probably one from his ship. A search by the captain proved that it had been removed from the crew mess room by the prisoner, who had told his mess mates that it had to be taken ashore to be cleaned, because it was not keeping good time.

The result was that the prisoner was charged with the theft. He duly appeared at the Thames Police Court and was fined ten pounds or one month in prison. The fine was paid by the ship's Captain; the prisoner left the court with the Captain, and the clock was returned to his ship.

John had a good run of similar successes after this, and his sergeant at Leman Street took a personal interest in his progress. He told him that he would have to study criminal law to become successful as a detective, and handed him a huge tome of printed matter entitled *The Metropolitan Police Guide*. This book contained the smallest print John had ever seen, and he was grateful that his sight was first-class. He was told to study this book at home, whenever he had spare time.

He thanked the Sergeant for the book, and assured him that he would read up on the contents as much as he could. This apparent enthusiasm undoubtedly pleased the Sergeant, who immediately told John that the book contained so much law that he should only read up on such aspects as The Larceny Acts, The Offences Against the Person Act, The Vagrancy Act, and the Metropolitan Police Act.

John certainly took this advice to heart, to the extent

that many of his colleagues would come to him and ask him about the powers of arrest in certain circumstances under a particular Act. This did not pass unnoticed by his superiors. In 1922, he was sent for by his Divisional Detective Inspector, who told him that his progress had been noted. Also, that he was now a Detective Constable of the Criminal Investigation Department. This, he was told, was not a promotion, just an advancement in the service, but if he continued in the manner that he had this far, he would soon be in a position of consideration for promotion.

These events took place at a time when John had found a more suitable flat in Shoreditch, on the top floor of Leopold Buildings, Columbia Road, quite close to Columbia Road School. The move was prompted by the fact that they would have a large bedroom, and also that when young John went to school, it would be only a short walk from home. Shortly after this, I commenced my schooling in the infants class at Columbia Road School.

My first clear recollections of that time are of learning that my father was a policeman, and I questioned my mother as to why he never wore a uniform. She told me that he was a detective, but at the same time not to tell my friends in the buildings, because not everybody likes being friendly with a detective or his family.

Life in those far-off days was good, and we were a very happy family. One less happy incident, however, still comes back to me from time to time. I recall my father coming home from work one evening with very red bleary eyes. He looked as if he had been crying. This made me very sad, particularly when mother started telling my father that he was drinking too much.

Noticing my apparent sad looks, they both came over

to comfort me. They seemed happy once again, and I was most relieved. I learned that my father and some of his colleagues had been out to raid the home of some thieves, and had been pelted with 'Pepper Bombs' (prepared paper bags of pepper) by the occupants. The thieves were all arrested, but the pepper had taken its toll, resulting in all of the officers having to have their eyes washed out at the station by the Police doctor, after they had brought in their prisoners.

It was at about this time that I was presented with a younger brother, Kenneth Eric SWAIN, born on 18th November 1925. We were a very happy family in our top floor flat in Leopold buildings, but the arrival of my little brother produced a problem that had to be solved. We now needed an extra bedroom, a matter that was promptly attended to by my father, who found a vacant flat at number eighty Leopold buildings, on the first floor, a few yards along Columbia Road, towards Hackney Road.

My father's occupation was, to my surprise, well known to my schoolmates when I commenced schooling at Columbia Road School. I also became used to being stopped as I was leaving the school to go home by members of other classes. The reasons were always the same: my father had arrested the father of the boy who stopped me, and a fight would start. This, thankfully, was always a one-to-one affair, with no outside interference like kicking or the use of a stick or implement. Furthermore, the duty teacher in the playground never attempted to stop the fight immediately, he just waited until the time was right.

I mentioned one of these incidents to my father; he just laughed and said something like, "So long as it was a fair fight, and you were not hurt. What do you expect?

This is the East End of London." I told him that although we had a Physical Training class at school, we did not get boxing lessons, yet most of the boys were better at it than I was.

"Come with me," he replied, as he got out of his chair. This came over more as a direct order than a simple request – but my father had been a Drill Sergeant in the Scots Guards during the war, so most of his requests came over as an order to be obeyed there and then. I was learning fast.

Once out of the flat, we climbed one flight of stairs to the roof, then walked along the roof to the next flight of stairs and went down to a flat on the same level as ours. I knew the occupant as Mr. Bone, a uniformed Constable serving at the Old Street Police Station. He opened the door. As Bert Bone, he was a well known and respected Police Boxing Champion, and his son (also Bert) and I were very good friends.

My father opened up the conversation. "Young John here is having a spot of bother with some of the sons of people I have nicked. He has also found out the hard way that he knows next to nothing about boxing. Just thought that you might have some bright ideas that could put him out of his misery."

I was not so sure that I liked that part of his speech, but I was keen to learn and who better than Mr Bone to teach me?

"No trouble," replied Mr Bone. "If he wants to learn, I will teach him. He will have to learn to take a few knocks, but that is all part of the training, Jock."

At that point my father decided to leave me to the tender care of his friend. I was told to sit down and listen to what Bert had to say. There followed a most interesting lecture incorporating what he referred to as 'The Marquis of Queensbury Rules': to always fight fair, irrespective of what method the other party may choose to use; to always remember the principal target areas, the chin, the nose and the Solar Plexus; and always hit hard – boxing is not a game.

He then told me to stand up, and showed me how to stand, with my right hand held in front of my chin, and my left hand extended forward slightly. I had to hit with the left hand, he said, and to use the right hand to parry off blows to the head or body. He then called over my friend Bert, who had been sitting on the other side of the room. Mr Bone then said to him 'Ready', and Bert immediately stood in the manner that Mr Bone had instructed me earlier. I watched the instructions as they were given and acted upon. I was most impressed – there was so much to learn about the 'simple' art of boxing.

I spent the evenings of the following two weeks on the roof of the flats whenever possible. I had with me either my friend Bert, or his father, whose instructions I followed closely. I was even asked to make one quite solemn promise: if anyone threatened to hit me, I was to hit them first, on the nose, not to just stand and wait for them to hit me. At first I found this difficult to accept. However, I respected Mr Bone, and waited for the next boy to try his luck with me.

I did not have to wait long. I was stopped at the gate by one of the older boys as I was leaving for my midday lunch. He stood in front of me and pushed me by the shoulder saying, "Put 'em up, Copper". I did, and hit him a nice one on the nose with my left fist before he could hit me. He reeled back, holding his nose, with his eyes running. His friends who were with him went over to him to comfort him, and I heard them saying, "Well, you did ask for it. You started it." Word soon got around the school that I was not one to take liberties with, and I had no further trouble at that school.

Mr Bone got to hear about this incident, and sent Bert over for me. He was pleased that I had responded in the manner that I had, and hoped that I would always remember his advice. I was now entitled to one other piece of advice that was even more important. "Just because you seem to be able to give a good account of yourself, don't ever start a fight. If you do, you will meet someone who is far more experienced and clever than you, and you will get a terrible beating. Now promise me, son." I made that promise, and looking back it was such sound advice. Advice that I have proudly followed throughout my life.

My father took his reading up on law seriously, as he did his work. He earned quite a reputation for being able to run faster than the local criminals – not that he gave them a chance to run, but when they managed to run off, he always caught them. That is, except for once!

Nineteen twenty-six was a bad year for strikes and work- place violence. It was also an unlucky year for my father. He was patrolling a trouble spot in the Limehouse area, where break-ins were rife, when he saw a man leave some office premises. He knew this man as a convicted thief, and went over to arrest him. The man saw him and ran off. Turning into East India Dock Road, the man jumped into a passing tramcar. My father caught up with the tram, and climbed on board. The man had run up to the top deck, so he climbed the stairs, only to see the man run down to the forward stairs and jump off the tram. My father followed and jumped off close behind as they arrived at the junction with West India Dock Road. He was very close to his quarry when he ran down the steps of the gents' toilet at this junction.

The next thing he knew, however, was nearly a week later. He was in the London Hospital, suffering from a depressed fracture of the skull. He had slipped on a date stone as he ran down the toilet steps after his quarry. The imprint of that date stone remained on the heel of his shoe for many years after that unfortunate incident.

John Swain

CHAPTER 3
THE FIRST PROMOTION

The obvious trauma at home needs no enlargement. Bessie had the care of the two boys, and everything else to worry about, including no money and rent to pay. Fortunately, fathers' colleagues came to her assistance with both his wages and advice. She visited him in hospital, and learned that he would soon be discharged, and found a place in the Police Nursing Home at Hove in Sussex. It was three weeks before he was released from the Nursing Home, and returned to Shoreditch.

There, by way of continuing his rest, he spent his off-duty time studying for a forthcoming promotion examination. He duly passed that examination, and was told that he would be posted as a Second Class Sergeant to Lavender Hill Police station in Battersea, on "W" Division. He was therefore advised to find himself the necessary accommodation, as he was expected to reside on the grounds of his new Division.

To John this seemed to be an enormous task, but to his surprise, within a day or so he had found a lovely flat in Sisters Avenue, quite close to Clapham Common. Nice as the nearby Common was, he wanted a garden, but here we occupied the first floor of the house, and the garden was out of bounds to us.

As for me, I now attended Wix Lane School, and met up with a new group of schoolmates. It was interesting , however, because they all seemed to know a lot about country ways, whereas I had never had the opportunity to walk about regularly on grass, and wander over such large fields as this. They also knew so much about the names of the trees, and some even went fishing for sticklebacks. I wanted to know more about that.

Even the school was more interesting here. My teacher, Mr Cox, was a former soldier from the Great War, and very much like my father. I got on well at my new school, and even enjoyed it. My father's work as a detective was respected, and I faced no hostility or trouble as I had in Shoreditch.

After nearly a year at our first Sisters Avenue address, my father found a flat in the same road that was considerably larger, with a nice large garden at the rear. With this flat came a huge mahogany table which, with the aid of a handle like a car starting handle, could be wound out and extra leaves inserted on it. This, I was told, was going to be turned into a table tennis table.

It was not long before I got into fishing for sticklebacks on the Mount Pond on Clapham Common, and I occasionally walked as far off as Wandsworth Common for the same purpose. I was surprised to find my father taking such an interest in my stickleback fishing. That is, until he told me to get up very early one morning, and took me to Teddington fishing on the River Thames. There he produced his Greenheart trout rod, and showed me how to use a real fishing rod. For me this was a most surprising experience, and one that undoubtedly infused me with considerable enthusiasm to take up angling myself.

Following that memorable trip to Teddington, I was always attempting to get my father to talk to me about his past angling experiences in Scotland before the war. He always made those talks so interesting, because they were personal accounts that rang so true.

Then came my seventh birthday, when he gave me a beautiful fishing rod and all of the accoutrements that went with it. This made me very happy, and that little rod lasted me many long years.

This was also the time when my father purchased a motor car. It was a Fiat open tourer and he promised to take the family to all manner of places. Our first trip was to Kenley, to visit my mother's sister Nettie. There I met my cousin John. He was a little older than I, and much bigger. Thus he became known as Big John, and I was called John-John.

The countryside around Kenley was so beautiful. We all used to go for long walks in the area, and I managed to increase my knowledge of plants, and birds, with rabbits in abundance, and Big John's dog Gyp chasing them, but never managing to catch one.

On one occasion here my father and Uncle Jack were discussing their work, and I heard my uncle tell the story of how he had captured a much wanted burglar named 'Gimlet Jim', for which he had received a Commissioner's Commendation. I was quite fascinated with the story of how, armed only with a carpenter's gimlet, this man had made a living raiding country cottages which in those days were rarely locked, or left locked. He would bore a hole above the latch lever, insert a wire loop or rabbit snare into the hole, lift up the latch, enter and steal whatever he fancied.

For my father, the larger rooms of the latest flat in Sisters Avenue were a boon. We would regularly have two or three of his colleagues visiting. On such occasions they would be poring over that huge book I have mentioned, *The Metropolitan Police Guide.* They would spend the whole evening asking each other questions from it, and discussing points of law and procedure. During these study periods, my brother and I were kept out of the way, and forbidden to make any noise.

Thankfully, even my energetic father had to have some rest. The old Fiat motor came to the rescue. On a day off duty, he would always find a nice place to take the family for a picnic. His favourite place was on the River Thames at Lalham Ferry, where he could park his car on the grass beside the river, and we could sit by the river and fish for Roach and Bleak. There, my mother would remain in the car with my brother Ken. She would generally spend the time knitting me a pair of socks, while Ken would be asking her all manner of questions.

I recall on one of those trips seeing my father talking to himself. I asked him what he was talking about. He laughed and said that he had to learn parts – definitions – of law parrot fashion, and was committing them to memory. They always came up in the Police Examinations and the various acts of parliament and definitions had to be written down without error. He laughed and said that he wanted to assure me that he was not going crazy, and the only way he could instil such matter in his mind was to repeat it either aloud or silently – preferably aloud, and this was an ideal opportunity, with nobody else listening.

The fishing went well, and I caught as many fish as my father. This was because I was paying strict attention to my line and float, while he was concentrating on his study. During the ride home, I learned that my father was going to sit a further promotion examination during the following weeks, and my brother and I had to keep out of the way and not disturb him and his colleagues, who would be coming to the house to study with him.

The time of the examination came and went. There was no more mass study visits. The family seemed quite relaxed, and I was told simply that my father now had to wait to hear whether or not he had passed the exam.

It was during this period that I noticed my father still spent a lot of time reading his big book in his favourite armchair. Probably noticing my attention to this, he told me that he thought it was time I started doing more reading. He told me to go to the public library just off Lavender Hill, join and take out a book on a subject that interested me.

I did as I was told, and borrowed my first book, an adventure story by T.C.Bridges. My father expressed an interest in the book, and I was worried in case I had selected the wrong type of book. His answer was that any book that interested me was good reading matter, because from reading the work of established authors, you learn how to spell and how to compose sentences correctly. He continued by telling me that in his work, the most important part of it was to be able to put everything he did into writing. His superiors had to read what he had written, and if his spelling and grammar were wrong, they would send it back to him just as if he was at school.

"Therefore, son, you must read as much as you can, good books, not comics, and your schooling will improve," he told me. "Then when you do leave school, you will be able to impress your boss with your written ability in whatever you take up by way of employment."

How grateful I was for the sound advice and words of

wisdom that were always forthcoming from my father. It was advice that came over in a quite a matter-of-fact way, not like the bullying efforts of some of our teachers. They always seemed to want to frighten you into doing something, an attitude that always made me more stubborn and unwilling to conform.

The more I thought about my father's approach, inviting me to progress with my study, the more I began to look upon him rather as a psychologist than a teacher. When he directed me to do something, it came over as an order, in line with his disciplinary training, and I jumped to it. On the other hand, when he wanted me to do something that he thought was for my benefit, it came over in a quite different manner, as with his suggestion that I joined the local library.

Then came a day in the early 1930s when excitement was prevalent in the house. My father had passed the examination, and had been selected to serve as a First Class Detective Sergeant on the Scotland Yard Flying Squad.

CHAPTER 4
ANOTHER STEP UP THE LADDER

My father's future activities here on would not be confined to a Divisional Area. As an officer on the Flying Squad, he could work anywhere within the Metropolitan Police District. Additionally, he could now live anywhere within that vast area – a subject that brought out much talk between my parents.

The family had learned to enjoy the countryside, particularly around Kenley and Caterham, but that, according to my father would be going out too far. Finally the builders Wates were found to be building some very nice houses at Norbury, perhaps halfway between Westminster and Caterham.

Thereafter, all talk was about money. The freehold of such a house came to just over four hundred pounds, and gathering in the necessary deposit was their next problem. The deposit was found, and the family moved out to Brockenhurst Way, Norbury, to a terraced house with a nice small garden backing on to a recreation ground. I went off to another school, Rowan Road, School, while my brother Ken went to Sherwood Park School.

The first big surprise came when my father arrived home from work in a large Bentley motor car. He was truly enjoying his Police work!

At Norbury I joined the local Boy Scout Troop, Doctor Palthorpes Own, the 96th Croydon Troop. I even enjoyed the drills and discipline, and became adept at Morse Code and Semaphore. On this point, however, I had a shock coming. Having told my father that I was good at Morse Code, he invited me outside the house on his return home one evening. In the back of a large Lagonda motor car that he was using sat a man with earphones on. My father sat me in the back with him and told me to read the Morse. It was far too fast for me, and just burbled away. I told him, and he said that they only employ former Royal Navy radio operators, and the Morse is too fast for anyone except an expert to read.

My father's work at this time concerned the fight against the Smash & Grab Raiders. It had become almost a fashion amongst certain thieves to use fast cars, drive up to a jeweller's shop, throw a heavy object through the shop window, grab trays of rings and other expensive items, and make off at a fast rate. As a result, the authorities decided that Bentleys, Lagondas, Lea Francis, Alvis, and other such vehicles were needed to combat this menace, and supplied them. They were most successful, and finally put down this form of criminal activity.

During this period John joined his colleagues in many exciting car chases and raids. On one such occasion, he was patrolling with his Detective Inspector, Gerry Lynch, in Mayfair. Whilst in Grafton Street, they heard the sound of breaking glass. Looking towards Bond Street, they saw a man running away from the scene They got out of their car and chased him. John grabbed the man, Sidney Farrell, a struggle endued, and they both crashed through the plate glass window of a shop. When arrested, Farrell said, "I am dead unlucky, if you had not been there, I would have got away." They went over to Garrards premises, and found the shop window smashed, with a brick lying inside.

They took Farrell to Vine Street Police Station, where he was charged with stealing a diamond and pearl bracelet valued at £175, the property of Garrards the jewellers of Albermarle Street Mayfair. He said, "I have been caught fair and square, I must put up with it. But I do ache." Subsequently, he appeared at Magistrates Court and was remanded in custody for a week. He was later dealt with at the County of London Sessions.

It was about this time that John Swain was recommended for promotion to Detective Inspector. Needless to say, he was delighted, but not a little troubled by the fact that he could not see himself remaining on the Flying Squad, because there were no vacancies there. Furthermore, with his home roots now established in Norbury, his feelings were that he would be once again obliged to move house.

He watched the postings regularly until the day when he noted that he had been posted to "H" Division, his original division in the Metropolitan Police, and he was instructed to report to Ted Nunne, the Divisional Detective Inspector in charge of that division. He was not sad at this posting, just a little worried, because he now had to find accommodation near to his work once again. The greatest worry, however, was that he would now have to let the house at Norbury that he was buying. He did not want to sell it, but retain it for his ultimate retirement.

He cast his net around, and located a house in Latham Road, East Ham. This he rented and made arrangements for my schooling at Altmore Avenue School, and my brother Ken's at Latham Road School. The move went well with one notable exception.

Whilst at Norbury, my mother had purchased a new and then modern Regulo gas cooker which she was very proud of. Here at East Ham there was a very ancient and dirty piece of history. She telephoned the gas company to ask them to remove it, but got nowhere with them. She then got my father to disconnect it, after which I assisted him to take it out of the house, and place it on the pavement outside. At this stage, the helpers deserted ship. Ken and I went off to school, and Dad went off to his work.

On our return, all was well. Mother had contacted the Gas Company and told them that their gas stove was outside on the pavement awaiting their pleasure. The gas men duly arrived, and she managed to induce one of them to connect her beloved gas stove for her. A happy ending all round.

It was not long after getting established at Arbour Square Police Station, the chief station on "H" Division, that my father became involved in a full scale murder investigation at the Palace Cinema, Bow. In this case Detective Chief inspector Nutty Sharpe of the Yard was called in to assist. It was established that Dudley Henry Hoard, the cinema manager, had been struck with an axe by nineteen-year-old John Frederick Stockwell, who had disappeared. Stockwell was traced to Yarmouth, and arrested by Chief Inspector Sharpe. When told that he would be arrested for the offence of striking Mr Hoard on the head with an axe, he replied, "The only thing I can say sir, is that I did not intend to kill him."

While the Stockwell case was between hearings, John was kept busy on all manner of work. He did, however, manage to take a day off work on Friday 27th September,1935, and take the family to Kenley to visit Jack

McPhail and family.

This was a time when two men, William McDonald of Bow, and Albert Arthur Wilkins from Whitechapel, were engaged in stealing the car of Mr Wally Segal. They were also being followed by a Police car containing Detective Constable Burr, and P.C. Veitch. When cornered, McDonald and Wilkins got out of their vehicle and ran, closely followed by the officers, who soon caught up with them. Then, as they passed a public house in the Mile End Road, one of the prisoners called out to those drinking on the pavement, "Get these bleeding coppers off me!"

The officers seized the two men, and were then harassed by the mob from the public house. At that moment, John Swain and family arrived on the scene. My brother Ken and I were ordered to climb over into the front seats with mother, and the men and their prisoners got into the back seat. The Morris Oxford Saloon certainly accommodated a load that it had not seen before, and stood up to it well. At Arbour Square Police Station the Police and prisoners were all off loaded, we rearranged ourselves, and continued on our way home to East Ham.

Shortly after that rather unusual experience, I left school, I had no idea where I would work, or just what I would do. As to skills, I had none. I did know, however, that when the time was right, I was going to be a Police Officer. The trouble was that my ambition had unfortunately become common knowledge at school. Gerry Crawley, one of my classmates called me a Copper's Nark. He ignored my request to refrain from calling me that name, so I hit him on the chin and knocked him down.

The headmaster got to hear of this incident, and sent for us. He made us both apologise, shake hands, and forget the matter. This we agreed to do in front of him.

Prior to my leaving school, the teachers went to a lot of trouble to sort out what type of work I should take up, and what would suit me. I had never been required to take an examination at school to qualify me for higher education. The headmaster expressed satisfaction with the work I had completed, but could only suggest that I applied for a position as a junior clerk or office boy. He gave me the address of the local Labour Exchange, and wished me good luck before shaking my hand at the end of the interview.

The following morning, as a fourteen year old I made my way to East Ham Labour Exchange, and stood in line for about an hour. I was given the name and address of a firm of Chartered Accountants in Moorgate, in the City of London. I made my way there, and arrived at midday. The Office Manager, Mr Alport, was very pleasant indeed. As for me I was a bag of nerves, although I did find some similarity of general attitude between Mr Alport and my father.

"Could I use a plug-in telephone exchange?" he asked. I assured Mr Alport that I had never used one, but could soon learn. My answer proved satisfactory, and I was told to come to the office at nine the following morning, and to report first to Mrs Gardiner. The wages would be twelve shillings and sixpence a week. "You finish work at five o'clock," Mr Alport said, then took me over to a large desk by the entrance door, with the old plug-in telephone exchange behind it. This was where I would work, and one of my tasks would be to answer the telephone, ensuring that all callers were attended to promptly and politely.

I arrived at nine sharp the following morning. Mrs Gardiner was waiting for me, and proceeded to outline my duties. First she told me that I should have arrived at the office at half past eight, not nine o'clock. She would speak to Mr Alport about that – "He should have known better," she said. The two partners and Mr Alport did not get in before nine, but my first jobs had to be completed before they arrived.

First I had to tidy up the desks of the three principals: change the blotting paper in their desk pads, sharpen pencils, check and exchange nibs in their pens where necessary, and top up ink wells. Needless to say, these simple tasks were no problem, and I soon settled down to the small plug-in telephone exchange.

The next task I had to master was using the very ancient means of copying company business correspondence. All letters reports and accounts had to be copied into a large, flimsy-paged copy book. Finally, at the end of the day, I had to enter outgoing mail into a large post book, apply stamps where necessary, and when I left the office, take the outgoing mail with me to the nearby post office.

This was a simple enough job. I could see no future in it, however, further than that I could end up as a fully paid clerk, checking over the figures of the principal accountants. Nevertheless, the general atmosphere was good, and I quickly began to enjoy the work, and seemed to get along well with all of the staff. I was also happy because at least I could learn something about accounts, a very useful subject that I knew so little about. I continued with my work, such as it was, and felt that I was able to satisfy everyone with my efforts.

At the end of my first week, Mrs Gardiner handed me my first week's wages, twelve shillings and six pence, which she placed in a small sealed envelope. I placed the envelope in my inside jacket pocket, and felt very good indeed. That night, I was as proud as punch that I was at last a wage earner, and able to produce something, small as it might be, towards the housekeeping.

Mother greeted me with a smile and a hug. I drew the envelope from my pocket as I walked over to the fire-place. The glow of the fire looked so warm and inviting, particularly as my hands were rather cold. I could feel the five half crowns inside the envelope making up the twelve shillings and six pence due to me. Keeping the coins in one half of the envelope in my hand, I tore the envelope in half and threw the empty half into the fire. Then, turning proudly towards mother who was standing on the other side of the kitchen table, I tipped out the coins in front of her.

I immediately realised the error of my ways, as my mother let out a shriek of horror. In front of her on the table were four pennies and a two shilling piece, plus the torn half of a ten shilling note. In something of a panic, I turned and dived my hand into the fire, singeing it slightly, and recovered part of the burnt envelope and the other half of the ten shilling note.

Mother would only say that at least I was being paid what I was worth – two and four pence! Then she held out the burnt envelope and its contents, including the coins, saying, "Just you wait, my boy, until your father gets home. He will have something to say to you about this state of affairs. I am sure that he will get a stick to you this time. Just you wait and see."

My father arrived home at about ten o'clock that evening, and I had no idea what to expect, except my obvious entitlement to some form of just punishment. Happily, I knew that my father was always a fair man, and this thought put me somewhat at ease. As soon as she heard his key in the door, however, mother rushed to greet him, and tell him the bad news that she had obviously not imparted to him on the telephone earlier.

I sat in the kitchen waiting. I stood up when they came into the room. Mother threw the evidence she had retained on to the table, saying, "One week's work, what do you think about that. Huh!"

"What have you to say for yourself?" asked my father. I explained to him my actions and reasoning. He nodded as my story went on. Finally, holding up his hand to stop me continuing, he said, "Presumption is one of the greatest enemies of mankind, lad. So many of us are always prepared to just presume that something is right or the other way round!" At this point he stopped and I waited, turning over in my mind the wisdom of his words. How very right he was.

Turning to me once again, he said, "I want you to remember this incident for the rest of your life, son, and promise me you will never presume anything unless you have positive grounds to believe the matter under review to be right or wrong, by obvious, and where possible visual indication or evidence. In this case, you just presumed that there were five half crowns in the envelope. You did not see five half crowns, you just expected them to be there, not four pennies and a two shilling piece.

"Had you opened the envelope, you would have found one ten shilling note, a two shilling piece, and the four pennies. You would then have complained to the cashier at work who would have told you that two pence had been taken out as your National Insurance contribution. Never presume anything, lad – always investigate. That's why I am a successful detective."

He then spread out the two halves of the ten shilling note on the kitchen table. "You are lucky," he said. "The number on the burnt half of the note is not damaged. It is quite readable, and your mother will be able to get it replaced with ease either at the post office or the bank tomorrow."

Firm and well thought out words of wisdom and advice were always available from my father, and to the best of my recollection, I always took such words seriously. I thought very deeply about them, and left home the following morning, firmly intent on giving a good account of myself both to my employer and to my father.

Everything went well for about three months. Then, one fateful morning, I arrived a few minutes later than usual. I rushed round the offices doing my allotted tasks, and in my haste in Mr Hennell's office, I knocked over his large three-legged antique swing chair. One of the legs broke off, and I did not know what to do. I lifted up the chair and propped up the broken leg by pulling the carpet up to stop the leg sliding away. It looked good! At that moment I heard Mr Hennell arrive, and heard him talking to one of the staff outside by the entrance door. I hurriedly left the office and crept behind my desk, making myself look busy by turning papers over.

Suddenly I heard a loud crash. I looked up and saw Mr Hennell's door swinging backwards and forward. Then, to my horror, I saw Mr Hennell getting up from the floor. I knew exactly what had happened! He had sat down on his chair and somersaulted backwards, knocking open his swing door and landing on the floor in the main office.

As the florid-faced boss got up and advanced towards

me, I knew that what I had done was, to put it mildly, bloody stupid. Clearly I had no excuse, and it would have been equally silly of me to attempt to offer one. The boss was having some trouble getting words out. Then it came in syllables: "You- You- You- You're fired! Get out!"

I made my way to Mrs Gardiner's office, where I told her what had happened. She did not seem to want to believe me, and made me repeat the facts to her. Then, while I was going through the matter, she started laughing. She then pulled herself together and said, "Mr Alport deals with staff matters, you had better go and see him and get your cards. Then if Mr Hennell has really sacked you, you will have to go."

I made my way to Mr Alport's office, knocked and entered when requested.

"What have you to say for yourself, young man?" he demanded in a quite stern voice.

"Nothing, sir," I replied. I did not feel like denying the obvious.

He continued, "John, it is obvious that you knocked over the chair in Mr Hennell's office this morning, and propped it up by using that old carpet. He's as mad as hell, and you will have to go. What have you to say for yourself?"

I did not know what to say. I thought a lot, but was very confused and nervous. Finally, I said, "I am sorry, sir, but my big worry now is: will I get a reference for my next job?" "

"Tell your next employer to get in touch with me. You have been honest and hard-working, but what happened today is unforgivable, and you must always remember that. Here's your cards, and good luck, lad." With that he offered me his hand, we shook hands and I left.

I made my way home in something of a daze. I did not know what I was going to tell my parents. Excuses came to me by the dozen, but I was not one to lie to my parents, especially to my father. As for Mother, whatever I said to her about the matter I would be in the wrong, so the less said to her the better.

I took my time going home but, not being one for hanging around in the street, I was back at the house in about an hour after leaving Mr Alport. My mother opened the door to me, and with a look of fright on her face, cried out, "What the Dickens are you doing here?"

I was not sure what I should say to her. Clearly this was not going to be my day. "I'm, sorry," I said, "I have been sacked."

"What?" she shrieked, and then went into a tirade of abuse about my uselessness. "No person will ever want to employ you now. As for your father, he will soon come to his senses and realise that the best place for you would be in the army. They at least will make something out of you."

The abuse continued, but I had had enough. I left the house, and walked to Wanstead Flats, where I spent a few hours wandering around and considering the words of wisdom from my mother. I had often wondered why it should be that my mother always held out the army to me as a threat. In my heart, being a soldier was the next best thing to becoming a policeman, so her threat was always wasted on me.

I returned home at half past six that evening, not knowing what kind of reception I was going to meet. Fortunately my father was home, and greeted me with a smile. "What do you think of this man's world now, lad?" he asked. I told him that I was not happy, but that what had happened was my own fault, although I still felt that if I had just reported knocking over Mr Hannell's chair and broken it, I would have met the same fate.

My father agreed with this contention, but to my surprise, added that as soon as he had heard from my mother that I had been sacked, he had telephoned Mr Alport and asked him what had taken place. He had been told about the damaged chair, and that it had been stupid of me to just prop it up in the hope that it would not come to light as his fault. Mr Alport had added that he had been very satisfied with my work, was sorry to see me go, and that when I obtained a further position, he would give me a reference accordingly.

I was then subjected to quite a long lecture on my activities, with particular accent on the fact that I must think before I acted again on the spur of the moment. This was very different from my mother's approach. It was a most sensible man-to-man chat, put together in few words with great meaning.

I pointed out to my father that during my recent cycle racing activities, I had met a man named Fred Stone, who worked for the Co-operative Wholesale Society in Leman Street, which had its headquarters at Aldgate. I told him that I was going to apply to them for a job, and he thought it was a great idea to obtain work with such an organisation.

So I applied for the job and, to my surprise, was accepted. I commenced work in the Post Room which was the place where they sorted out new members of their staff as they joined. From there, I was posted to work in the Ladies' Glove Department under a Mr Reader. There, I was given the job of 'City Boy'. This called for me to go in the City of London to the various large shops to find a type of glove ordered by a distant branch of the Co-op but not held in stock. This was interesting work, and I managed to save up enough money to purchase a proper racing cycle, and take up my chosen sport successfully.

With my savings, plus a little assistance from my father, I managed to buy a made-to-measure racing cycle frame. It was in the process of being made, and I would have to wait for about a month before it would be ready. In the meantime I joined a local cycle club. All went well until I had an unfortunate accident at High Beech in Epping Forest. Returning home in the dark after a club meeting, I struck a dog, and went careering over the handlebars. I literally bit the dust, and ended up in Loughton Cottage Hospital, having some nasty gashes in my face stitched up. My father collected me from the hospital, took me home, and I spent the following two or three weeks at home having the wounds attended to while they healed up. Not a nice experience at all.

My father at this time was offered accommodation in the married quarters of Bow Road Police Station. This involved another move, but we were getting used to such changes.

The accommodation above the police station was excellent, with quite large rooms and a fire escape from the bathroom to the station yard. The fire escape would be useful to bring my cycle up from the yard, where I would otherwise have been obliged to leave it.

In early 1937, John Swain was promoted to Divisional Detective Inspector, and posted to "N" Division, with his office at Stoke Newington Police Station. Life was certainly moving fast for the former farm labourer and Dundee Police Officer, and he was enjoying the challenge of each separate job as it came in.

Violence seemed to be the order of the day. He dealt with each case on its merits with his officers, and passed much of the final investigative work over to the trained detectives on his staff. The object of his actions was confined to close supervision, and ensuring that the correct action was taken in each case.

There were many such cases in 1937 and 1938, and I was aware that in each case my father went into available evidence thoroughly. We at home, the family, also became very much aware of the fact that he was working under constant heavy pressure. Such was the pressure that in early 1937, he decided to move house from the married quarters of Bow Road Police Station, to a terraced house in Comberton Road, Clapton, in order to be closer to his office.

That year a four-year-old girl, Beryl Osborne, was found bound and gagged and strangled in a sack in a shed in Hazellville Road, Upper Holloway. This was a shocking affair, for which her thirteen-year-old brother was responsible.

I had never before seen my father so disturbed by a case he was investigating. The final act of this terrible saga was played out at the Central Criminal Court in London. There the brother, who had sat beside his mother throughout the proceedings, was 'acquitted of murder, taken from his mother, and sent to an approved school'.

I was happy at the Clapton address, and managed to keep myself extremely fit with my cycle racing, I entered a number of twenty-five mile cycle races, and won several. In my spare time, I became involved with short wave radios, and even made a useful receiver, with which I made contact with people in other countries. By the time I was at the transmitter stage, however, the family was on the move again, and I had to abandon that idea.

In 1939, my father was transferred from "N" Division in North London to "A" Division, as the Divisional Detective Inspector, with his office at Cannon Row Police Station just off Whitehall. Serving at this Division, he was once again able to live anywhere within the Metropolitan Police District. For the family, this meant another move. Unfortunately, our old house in Brockenhurst Way, Norbury was still occupied by one of my father's colleagues, so we had to find another suitable house.

On 7th July 1939, the family moved from Clapton to Woodmanstern Road, Norbury, into a house with a nice garden that backed on to the Westminster Bank Sports Ground.

Around this time, my brother Ken joined the Benbow Sea Cadet Corps at Mitcham. Prompted undoubtedly by the general talk of imminent war with Germany, this was something that he took most seriously. He even studied Naval Gunnery to the extent that he became the Petty Officer Instructor in Gunnery of his group.

For me, the move back to Norbury was most pleasant. I was settled into my work at the C.W.S., and continued with my night school studies. This now included shorthand, which was slowly taking shape.

Then on a day in early August, I was awakened early in the morning by noises from the sports ground. Large guns where being wheeled into the centre of the field. There had been much talk at work about the probability of imminent war with Germany, and my immediate thought on seeing those guns was: 'Surely they are not going to invade us?'

One memorable day in my family history is 30th August 1939. That day I sat a shorthand examination to obtain the necessary eighty words a minute certificate to get me into the Metropolitan Police as a Divisional Shorthand Writer. I entered the school hall where this was to take place full of confidence – I had quite recently passed a one hundred and twenty words a minute test in the same hall. But within a minute, I found that the examiner was running away from me. Shorthand is an exact and positive writing science, and it was not possible to catch up with the examiner. I failed the test, and left the premises absolutely devastated.

Back home at Woodmansterne Road, my mother greeted me with a smile and said, "You passed, I am sure." Or something like that. I lowered my head and admitted my failure. She immediately launched into one of her familiar tirades about my inability to do anything. I was useless. I would never get into the Police. The only place for me was in the army. They at least would make something out of me.

I did not wait for her to finish. I turned and walked back down the garden path to the roadway, turned and made my way to Norbury Police Station. There I asked the Sergeant for the addresses of the nearest recruiting offices. He gave me details of The London Welsh Regiment of Mitcham Lane, Streatham, and The Royal Army Service Corps, Mitcham Road, Croydon.

CHAPTER 5
I JOIN THE ARMY.

Still very downcast at my failure, I left the station and walked to Mitcham Lane, Streatham. There I was met by a charming gentleman wearing an officer-type superfine uniform and a Sam Brown belt, who offered me his hand and said something like, "So you want to join the army, lad? You are just the type we are looking for", and ushered me into the premises.

I was handed over to a man wearing a Royal Army Medical Corps flash on his shoulder, to have a medical examination. He pronounced me A1 in fitness, but I have no idea how he came to that conclusion. I then went to another office where another officer was sitting behind a desk. A very short ceremony took place that I have no recollection of right now, but at the conclusion, the officer leant across, shook my hand, and said, "Congratulations, young man, you are now 1478572 Gunner John Swain of The 99th London Welsh Regiment, Royal Artillery."

At this stage, the first gentleman I had met me tapped me on the shoulder and escorted me out of the premises, informing me that I should report to the Westminster Bank Sports Ground at 9am the following day, and warned me not to be late. I told him that I thought I had joined the Royal Army Service Corps. This seemed to shock my friend, who stiffened and said something like, "You are now in the London Welsh Regiment, the finest regiment in the British Army, and don't you forget it."

I was proud to be in the army, but extremely worried about what my father would say when I got home and told him I had joined a Welsh regiment. He was such a proud Scot. With this thought worrying me, I entered the house. My father was sitting with my mother, and I thought I would jump in at the deep end, so I said, "I've joined the army, Dad, I am now a Gunner in the London Welsh regiment, and have to report over the back here at nine tomorrow morning."

Mother burst into tears, and I apologised to my father for joining a Welsh regiment. He got up and patted me on the back saying, "Don't worry lad. Whatever regiment you are serving in has to be the best in the army. A soldier without pride in his regiment is only of use to the enemy. I was in The Scots Guards. It is still the finest regiment in the army to me, and always will be."

I reported to the Orderly Room in the pavilion of the sports ground behind the house as directed at nine the next morning. There I was fitted out with a uniform complete with brass buttons, and everything from a greatcoat to a button stick. I was then taken to a large hut, shown how to lay out my kit, and where to sleep when directed to. Quite obviously, the army had reorganised what was a sports pavilion into what to my inexperienced eye seemed to be an efficient centre of activity, complete with a quartermaster's store and canteen.

There followed periods of drill. First came foot drill under Battery Sergeant Major Giles. There were about eight of us recruits, and our Sergeant Major had quite a task knocking us into shape. To a man, we came away with the impression that he was a bit of an actor, but we also admired his patience, which at times seemed to be near breaking point.

Then there was the gun drill that was quite obviously so very important. There we learned that the guns were controlled by a group of instruments in a command post situated in the centre of the four guns. The Heightfinder first locates the distance and height of the incoming plane, and passes that information to the Predictor. This genius calculates the position and speed of the plane, and works out what fuse to fire at a given height, and transmits a specific bearing and angle for the gun layers to follow. All this after taking into consideration the barometric pressure at mean sea level. Once all of these considerations have been worked out, the final act is in the hands of the Command Post Officer, who gives the fuse instructions and orders the guns to fire – this in the sincere hope that the predictor had worked out accurately where the plane will be when the shell reaches this vague altitude, explodes and shoots down the plane.

To us, this was all a complete mystery, but as we listened to the lectures from those who were supposed to know all about anti-aircraft fire, it became a subject that we all took a personal interest in.

The next surprise came when we were all told to pack our kit and get into The Royal Army Service Corps lorries that had arrived at the camp. There had been plenty of rumours as to what we were going to do in the future, but we dismissed most of them as what was then referred to as 'latrineographs'. One such rumour was that we would be going to Aberporth in Wales to a firing camp.

It was therefore no big surprise when we arrived at Paddington Railway Station and were directed to a train, and sure enough made our way to Aberporth. We arrived at a railway station at Newcastle Emlyn. There civilian lorries were waiting for us to take us to Aberporth. That ride to Aberporth was somewhat frightening. It is a hilly area, and the lorries would grind their way up a hill, and on reaching the top, the driver would knock the gear lever into neutral, and coast down the other side of the hill at an extremely fast pace. We were, to a man, most relieved when we arrived at our billet, and relaxed after that quite scary ride.

We spent very little time in Aberporth itself. We were there for a reason, and our days were taken up either with lectures, or we were taken to a location high above the town overlooking the sea. There we started gun drill with a vengeance, and were told that we were good at our job as gunners. This surprised us somewhat because the army rarely compliments anyone unless they are truly worthy of it and, being honest amongst ourselves, we did not think we were that worthy.

A plane came over the firing camp towing what we were told was a 'sleeve', a long cloth tube. We commenced our drill to the complete satisfaction of the Instructor of Gunnery in charge. He told us that we were now entitled to fire live rounds. The fusing and loading went according to the orders, and the layers put the guns on their bearing and angle positions as directed. All went well until one shell exploded immediately beneath the towing plane. There were hoarse shouts of "Cease firing!" coming from the Command Post, and everything stopped.

The widespread confusion that followed had us all worried. From the era of compliments we now became a rabble of quite useless individuals. Then, whilst this was going on, we noticed that the towing plane had released the sleeve, and was flying directly at us, oh so very low. We all ducked out of the way.

Of course, being soldiers we had to have our own

court of enquiry. It was all very well the Gunnery Instructor telling us how useless we were, but some of us, those not concentrating on their respective dials, had watched the incident. Four guns were firing, and only one shell had exploded under the plane. The other three had exploded under the sleeve, as they were supposed to. Our impression was that perhaps there had been a fault in the wiring from the Command Post to the offending gun, but when we tried to get this message over to those in charge, we got nowhere. All we were told was that some 'bloody fool' had taken his eyes off his dial and probably thought that he was supposed to fire at the plane. The final statement was that all guns and instruments were controlled by a three-phase A.C. circuit that was still in perfect working order. Something had obviously gone wrong, but we, the scapegoats, felt that there was more to it than the feeble excuse given by those in charge. Resigned, we decided that we were, and intended to remain, good soldiers; we let the matter rest at that, swearing to be more careful in the future.

Returning to our original location at Westminster Bank Sports Ground, I read a request on the Battery Notice Board, asking for volunteers to be dispatch riders. This sounded like a job for me. I had never ridden a motorcycle, but my balance was good after riding cycles for so long. I could drive a car, so I felt that without much difficulty, I could also ride a motorcycle. I applied for the job and got it, after assuring the Orderly Room Sergeant that I could ride a motorcycle. I was given a cheque for thirty pounds and told to get the then current dispatch rider, Gunner Downes Powell, to take me to the Pride & Clarke premises at Brixton and buy a motorcycle. All the way to Brixton, I watched closely the control actions of Downes Powell, and on arrival at the premises, I was quite sure that I could get whatever motorcycle I ended up with back to the regiment without difficulty.

We arrived in a yard at the side of the Pride & Clarke premises. There I handed the cheque over to a man who was obviously expecting army personnel to come and collect motorcycles. Indicating a line of bikes he said, "Help yourself, they're all the same price." I walked along the line, attempting to look knowledgeable, and selected a beautiful A.J.S. Silver Streak. I told the man to start it up, which he did. I then asked him to take it up the yard and back, making some excuse about the fact that it looked out of track. He shook his head, and did as asked.

On his return, I thanked him, got on the machine, and gently rode out of the yard into Stockwell Road. The machine seemed to be going well, and I was not going to take it out of first gear until I had the opportunity to practise in a quiet side road.

Downes-Powell was hopping mad and said, as we rode along, that he was going to report me because I obviously had no idea how to ride a motorcycle. I pulled into a side road near Streatham Tate Library, and spent about an hour practising with this machine, and finally thought I could get away with it. My colleague, however, was not so sure. He already had me pictured in the Guard Room. I did ride into camp past the guard and other watchers, and no adverse comment was made. In fact, I rode motorcycles throughout the war years successfully, and without mishap.

I was, of course, aware of the fact that I had to take my time and get used to traffic and the lighting in those days of the blackout. The main thing was that this job got me away from guard duty, fatigues and other military chores. It was also a stepping stone. I wanted to get a full driving licence, and drive army vehicles.

On this point, I should mention that when my father was stationed at Stoke Newington, he introduced me to the manager of the Manor House garage. This was close to Haringey Arena, and when there was a boxing match or other show going on there, I could go to the garage, and park cars for those who wanted to leave them with us while they went to the arena. Apart from the fact that I earned a few shillings towards paying for parts for my push bike, I was learning to drive and park accurately. I therefore knew that when I gained the opportunity to drive in the army, I would have no difficulty with the driving. Whilst I was working away attempting to become a good soldier, my father was beavering away at his important work as the Divisional Detective Inspector of the Royal "A" Division.

In March of that year, I took a friend to see a show at the Victoria Palace Theatre. It had been agreed that my father would meet us in the foyer of the theatre at 6.30pm. We arrived on time, but my father was not there. This was so unusual for a man who was always so strict on the timing of appointments. We asked for the manager. He had received a message from my father to say that he was busy, and could not get there to see us. The manager put us in some fine seats, and we watched the show.

When the show ended, one of my father's officers was waiting for me. He told me that my father had been engaged in a murder investigation, and would not see us that evening. We returned to camp, and I had to wait until the following morning before I discovered just what had detained him.

The facts of the case were that Sir Michael O'Dwyer,

Lieut. Governor of the Punjab during the Amritzar riots in 1919, had been shot dead the previous evening at the close of a crowded meeting of the East India Association in Caxton Hall, Westminster. He was seventy-six years of age. Three other men bearing famous names were wounded by revolver shots fired from the body of the hall by, it is alleged, an Indian. They were: Lord Zetland, aged 63, Secretary of State for India and Burma; Sir Louis Dane, aged 84, former Under-Secretary to the Governor of the Punjab; and Lord Lamington, aged 79, former Governor of Bombay.

The first shots struck Lord Zetland, who was on the platform. He fell from his chair, wounded in the arm. Sir Michael O'Dwyer, sitting in the front row close to the man with the gun, jumped to his feet, and made as if to tackle the man. Then he fell dead with two bullets in his body. A coloured man, Mohamed Azard Singh, was later charged with the murder and due to appear at Bow Street Magistrates Court later that day. Quite a story! A subsequent picture in the Daily Mail showed my father and some of his colleagues taking the man away from Caxton Hall. Mohanmd Azard Singh was later sentenced to death at the Central Criminal Court.

During this period I got on with my work as a dispatch rider, travelling between outposts of the regiment in south London. I followed the Caxton Hall murder closely, with a feeling of pride in my father as I read the press reports on this shocking affair. I became even more intent on my own future, and vowed that I would join the Metropolitan Police if I was lucky enough to see the war through without serious injury.

These were the thoughts that were passing through my mind as I returned from 48th Brigade Headquarters at

Lee Green in June 1940. Travelling along Brownhill Road, I changed down on my approach to Rushey Green. The road was clear from my right, and a tram was approaching from the left on the other side of the road. As I turned left, my machine slid from under me. There was a *Ping Ping Ping* as the tram driver struck his alarm bell. I managed to scramble off, but the bike slid nicely up into the Cow Catcher under the driver. With the aid of the tram driver and a passing motorist, we got the bike out, and I was pleased to see that there was little visual damage apart from a small scratch on the mudguard.

On my arrival back at camp, I learned that there had been a murder in Hyde Park, on my father's ground. My enquiries revealed that a War Reserve Police Constable, Jack William Avery, had been stabbed and taken to St Mary's hospital, Paddington, where he died. Also that Frank William Cobbett, a labourer, had been charged with his murder by Divisional Detective Inspector Swain. This man later appeared at the Central Criminal Court, and was sentenced to death.

It was at about this time in 1940, when I had listened to some officers of the Royal Army Ordnance Corps speaking about our guns. The talk was so interesting that I felt I should aim to get involved in the workings of the guns. As I saw it, the first step for me was to get the job referred to by the unbelievers as 'the greasy Monkey Job' of Limber Gunner. To me this was a strange job with the responsibility of ensuring that the guns were spotlessly clean and always ready for inspection or action.

I applied for this unusual job, and to my surprise got it. It seemed that few of my comrades had a desire to get their hands dirty, but the rewards were there to be collected: Limber Gunners were excused normal parade;

there was no guard or picket duty, and no specific time for the work to be done. Just get up at reveille, have your breakfast, then get on with the job on your gun, and go to bed only when that work has been completed satisfactorily.

From the quartermaster's store, I obtained the handbook on the 3.7"Anti Aircraft Gun, and spent much time reading and learning about the guts of this monster. It was so very interesting. Then I started taking the breech mechanism apart, and had quite a shock. I was always fairly good at taking objects apart, and putting them together again, but this was a very different subject. It took me a day before I was truly satisfied that everything was in its place, and together as it should be.

The shock came when the Orderly Officer came round on his inspection. He immediately opened up the breach, and started prodding about with his cane. As he closed the breach, he turned to me and said, "Excellent, the cleanest breach mechanism on the site. I saw you working away at it. Keep it up." With that, he turned and left. I dearly wanted to tell him that he should not prod my breach mechanism about with his damned cane, but thought better of it. Nevertheless, I could well imagine him striking the ejectors and having a half hundredweight of breach mechanism smashing his cane, if he continued on his rounds in this manner.

It was probably that officer's report that brought about my being sent to Shrapnel Barracks in Woolwich on a Gun Fitter's Course, my first step up the ladder in the army. This was an entirely new experience for me. Living in a military barrack block, and having to march, not walk, to the gun shop where the instructions were to be given. That quarter mile march was always a problem.

There were always young officers marching towards me on the way, who demanded a smart salute if what you gave them was not up to their standard. If it was, they usually commented on the fact that my boots were not shiny enough for their liking. All very frustrating!

The instruction received at the gun shop was excellent, given by regular soldiers, usually Artillery Sergeants who really knew their business. Then one afternoon whilst the Battle of Britain was going on in the skies above, there was an almighty crash with fragments of 'something' falling on the roof of our building. We looked outside, and all we could see was the tail of a Spitfire sticking out from a hole in the middle of the road. One of our RAF colleagues had not made it. We stood together in silent prayer for the brave fallen airman.

The week at Shrapnel Barracks taught us all a great deal about army life. As we discussed the day's work together during the evenings, we were, to a man, ever grateful for the experience gained.

In August 1940, I was sent to The Ascot Water Heater works at Letchworth in Hertfordshire on a fitter's course. First I had to settle in to a civvy billet, where I was looked after by a husband and wife who undoubtedly enjoyed the experience of being able to do their bit toward the war effort, although they were too old for active service. This was to be for ten weeks, during which time we were to be taught how to use all manner of simple engineering tools. We were soon aware that learning how to file flat was not something you picked up immediately; it was something that took years of practice, practice and more practice. We all tried hard, and somehow managed to convince those in charge that we were fit and proper people to be let loose on the army equipment that would be under our control as gun fitters.

The instruction went through all of the elementary uses of the file, the chisel, the drill, and the blacksmith's fire. I enjoyed every minute of the time, including the frustration of attempting to pass muster under the eagle eye of our Scottish instructor, who demanded nothing less than perfection. Though we did our best, he quite obviously believed it was *his* efforts had brought us up to his standard.

By the end of the course, my regiment had moved to a gun site in the sports ground of Finsbury Park. On my arrival, I was promoted to Full Bombardier. Clearly I had made the right choice in becoming a 'Grease Monkey cum Limber Gunner', and set about the work immediately. Shortly afterwards, I was promoted to Lance Sergeant, Battery Fitter, as we moved off to the defence of RAF Wattisham. There I enjoyed the privileges of being a member of the Sergeants' Mess, and all of the little extras that go with it.

The regiment once again had guns on various sites both within the perimeter of the airfield and in the surrounding countryside. My work here was to visit these sites, and ensure that the guns were working one hundred per cent satisfactorily all round.

Everything went well until one fateful morning. We had been quite regularly raided by a solitary Dornier Bomber of the LuftWaffe at eleven in the morning, by what was known as 'hedge hopping'. The plane came in at zero level, dropped a bomb somewhere in the airfield area and decamped. We waited at stand-by and heard a plane approaching. As it was sighted, we fired. It was no German plane, but an RAF Beaufort Bomber, and we took off the landing gear. Needless to say,, the wires were red hot after that.

CHAPTER 6
PROVOST SERGEANT

Wattisham was very interesting, and most time-consuming for me. The inspection of the guns became more intense after the unfortunate shooting down of the Beaufort Bomber. Then on one occasion, when I was returning from the Sergeants' Mess after breakfast with Sergeant Major Giles, he said, "What is this I hear about you intending to join the Police after this lot is over?"

"That is quite correct sir," I said.

"Then I've got a job for you today," came his reply. My thoughts were immediately: *Now what have I volunteered for?* Sergeant Major Giles continued by telling me that Gunner McDonald, who had joined the regiment at the same time as I had, had 'gone over the side', indicating either desertion or absent without leave

I had no idea which of these military offences he was guilty of, and the Sergeant Major did not seem to want to enlarge on the subject. Then he cut in on those thoughts. "Take Gunner Robson with you, I think he was supposed to have been a Special Constable, or something like that. McDonald is detained at Great Scotland Yard by the Military Police. You are now the Battery Provost Sergeant. There is no extra pay with the job. You get quite enough as the Battery Fitter."

Back at the billet, the Sergeant Major handed me his revolver and said, "You will need this. If he runs off, shoot him – he's a bloody deserter as far as I am concerned." Having noted that the revolver was loaded, I strapped it on. I had never worn a pistol before, and definitely had never fired one. I then located Bill Robson, and we were taken to Ipswich Railway Station, where we caught a train to London.

During the journey, I was turning over in my mind the words of the Sergeant Major. *Shoot McDonald.* I could not imagine that. In any event, I was not going to let him escape, so shooting would not be necessary. While the trauma of this matter was going through my mind, I remembered that my father was stationed at Cannon Row Police station, only a few hundred yards from Great Scotland Yard.

We called in on him, and he was delighted to see us. He questioned me at length on my new post as the Provost Sergeant. He then took us along to Great Scotland Yard and introduced us to Colonel Imrie, who was in charge of that Military Police Depot. This was a most useful introduction, and advanced my meagre knowledge of the military side of Police matters that would be of use to me in future years. We collected McDonald and returned to Wattisham without incident. I returned the pistol to Sergeant Major Giles, and he actually bought us both a drink in the canteen, an incident that could not pass without everyone present noticing.

The interesting part of that escort duty came out some weeks later, when I was called upon to give evidence of taking McDonald back to Wattisham. A Police Officer from Paddington Police Station gave evidence to the effect that McDonald had been in the Edgware Road when a bomb struck a building, trapping a number of people. McDonald had jumped in and started pulling people out. The Police Officers he had assisted then asked him to come to the station and have a meal. He would not do that because he had to get back to his regiment. They decided to take him to the station, and there discovered that he had overstayed his leave, and were obliged to inform the Military Police.

That month, December 1940, I recall reading in The Star newspaper of a case my father had been involved in. Patrick O'Flynn, a 24-year-old carpenter from Loftus Road, Shepherds Bush, had been stopped in the street, in possession of a silver gilt box and a silver gilt key. O'Flynn had been employed as a carpenter to repair windows at Buckingham Palace. He had forced a cabinet with a screwdriver at The Royal Palace Mews, and stolen these items. Then when his home was searched, two wallets were found that had also been stolen from the same place. At Bow Street Magistrates Court, he was sentenced to six months imprisonment.

January 1941 saw my regiment uprooted and taken to Euston Railway Station, thence to Perth in Scotland. We got off the train at Perth, and were put on a second train that ended up at Thurso. There we were loaded on to a ship that took us to Lyness in the Orkney Islands. From there, Regimental Headquarters and 303 Battery headquarters staff, and one troop of 303 Battery were dispatched to South Ronaldsay. There, at Herston point, I set up my fitters' workshop, and started my inspection of the guns we had taken over for the defence of the Scapa Flow naval base.

I thoroughly enjoyed my work at this location. I had to travel to other islands where troops of our battery were posted, carrying out repairs and inspections. It was all good interesting stuff. Then, periodically, I would be called upon to bring back to camp those who had overstayed their leave and fallen foul of the Military Police.

As to entertainment, we made our own, as soldiers

always do. We put on the odd play, with me supplying the lighting needed and the noises off! Additionally, I got in with a crofter and went out fishing with him, thus managing to supply the Sergeants' Mess with quite a lot of fresh fish. I was so happy and contented with my work that I could have stayed there with 303 battery until the end of the war, but that was not to be.

The Battery Captain, Captain Griffiths sent for me one morning to tell me that I had been posted to The Military College of Science at Stoke on Trent on an Armament Artificers' Course. He shook my hand and wished me luck. In truth, I did not want to leave the regiment, but he insisted that I go. Now, when I look back at that meeting, I cannot help but think just how lucky I was to have served under such a man.

I packed up my kit, said a fond farewell to all of the tools I had collected for my work, and climbed into a truck. Then as we drove out of camp, I bid a sad farewell to my regiment, and a location I had so thoroughly enjoyed serving. I caught a drifter at St Margarets Hope, to Lyness, from there the St Ninian and over a peaceful Pentland Firth, to Thurso. Then by train to Perth, Edinburgh, and on to Leicester. There I followed my Movement Order instructions to the Military College of Science.

To my surprise, the students were all either Sergeants, Staffs Sergeants, or Warrant Officers, while the instructors were mostly Officers or Class (1) Warrant Officers. The instruction was good, but there was a great deal to remember. Consequently, there were some who dropped out along the way, and I must say that I found the course anything but easy.

In March 1942, I was promoted to Staff Sergeant Royal

Army Ordnance Corps, and continued with dogged determination. Then in June of that year, the Major in charge of our class shook my hand and told me that I was now a Staff Sergeant Armament Artificer (Field), and gave me a Movement Order to report to the 2nd Infantry Brigade Workshops of the 1st. Infantry

CHAPTER 7
THE 2ND INFANTRY BRIGADE WORKSHOPS

At East Dereham in Norfolk, my welcome was most impressive. I was urgently needed to take over the Armament section of the workshop, and set about getting myself organised in this new post immediately. This was a time when the Royal Army Ordnance Corps was being completely reorganised. In fact, R.A.O.C. as such became a Field Park, gathering in and storing the equipment required principally by a new regiment being formed called The Royal Electrical and Mechanical Engineers. Additionally, I was promoted to Artificer Quartermaster Sergeant R.E.M.E.,Warrant Officer Class II, with the pay that went with the rank.

It was here that I truly began to appreciate the training I had received at the Ascot Factory in Letchworth. I was called upon to make parts in line with that training, and thankful that I had followed it up with my work as the Battery Fitter in the London Welsh. Now, when I took on a job myself, my men watched me closely, and I knew that I had to impress upon them that I was capable of doing the necessary work satisfactorily.

The scale of the workload soon gave everyone the impression that we were gearing up to travel overseas. Then we moved en-bloc to Kilmarnock in Scotland. Almost before the information from those who were supposed to know leaked out, we immediately started waterproofing our vehicles. We were so close to the River Clyde that the rumour-mongers could not resist telling us that they had decided that we were off to Norway. This rumour persisted until common sense and the position of certain guiding stars proved it wrong.

In January 1943, we boarded the SS Dunutter Castle at Gourock. We travelled due north, so Norway it had to be. Then when islands appeared on the port side of the ship, they told us that they were obviously the Orkneys, although many doubted that. Two nights later, with the North Star flickering away on the starboard beam, they had cracked it. We were off to the United States to link up with the Yanks and return with them to invade Europe. That silly rumour still existed the following morning, when we found that our solitary troopship had been joined by a number of similar ships plus a Royal Navy escort. That night, I was pleased to find the North Star on the Port side of the ship.

The following morning, I was unduly surprised to find that we were approaching Gibraltar and the destination choices became France, Algiers, Tunisia or Egypt.

We landed at Algiers, on 9th March, and then marched to Maison Carre where, quite exhausted, we camped overnight in a large barn, disturbed at times by the biggest rat ever seen by any of us. From there we moved off to a railway station, boarded cattle trucks and travelled east. Our next stop was Bone, where we took over a prepared transit camp – not for a rest, but just until our next train was ready to receive us. Yes, another Cattle Truck that took us as far as Bou Salem There waiting for us, courtesy of the Royal Army Service Corps, were our vehicles from far away Scotland. We were delighted to see them again, and made our way with them to nearby Teborsouk, where we set up our workshop. We could hear distant gunfire, and guns and vehicles started coming in for repairs almost as soon as we arrived.

The work was varied and interesting, but we did not remain in Teborsouk long before we were on the move east once again. Through Medjes El Bab to the edge of Tunis then to Souse, and on to Kelibia at the tip of Cap Bon. There our work was to get all of the Divisional equipment back into full battle order, for we were obviously contemplating a further move overseas, this time to the south of France or Italy. To me, it had to be Italy, and to that end, I started attempting to learn Italian with the aid of a Spanish fisherman named Batiste, who lived near our camp. This was an enjoyable but failed experience.

I had learned a lot of French in North Africa, though not particularly good French, because for the most part this was the result of conversations between myself and an occasional Arab. My interest in languages was such that I felt sure French and Italian would be of use to me if and when I got into the Police, when the war was over. I had at least kept up my shorthand by keeping my diary in shorthand, and taking down the odd lecture in shorthand when the opportunity presented itself.

On 17th January 1943, my brother Ken decided to leave the cadet force and join the Royal Navy as a Junior Rating. He signed on at the Royal Navy recruiting office in Poplar Walk Croydon. Subsequently, in April 1943, he went through a small ceremony on board H.M.S. Collinwood, was given the service number P/JX518343, and received the Kings Shilling.

He sailed on the Queen Elizabeth to NewYork, where he became engaged in all manner of naval training exercises leading up to the commissioning of H.M.S.Bickerton at Boston. From there they sailed to the West Indies and then on an ASDIC Course to The Falklands finally returning to Portland Maine and Bickerton. From there they sailed to Iceland and on to Belfast, where Bickerton joined a group of destroyers known as Group 5, of the Western Approaches Force, with Bickerton as the leader of the group.

The object of the group was to hunt the German U Boats that were harrying our shipping generally. Following this they sailed to the coast of Normandy to protect our shipping during the landings there. During this time two ships of the group were sunk. Bickerton returned to Scapa Flow and formed up with operation Goodwood, to attack the German Battleship Tirpitz.

During this operation, Ken was engaged as an after Oerlikon gunner and was so engaged when the ship was struck by an enemy torpedo, off the north or Norway in the Barents Sea. This took place at 5pm. on 22nd. August 1944, a date that Ken will never forget. The massive explosion that followed deafened Ken, badly affected his sight, and smashed his teeth. He was picked up by H.M.S Kempthorn and taken to Lyness in the Orkney Islands. He was then taken by ship to Thurso, followed by a long and tedious train journey to Portsmouth. There, after some treatment, he was given 21 days' leave, later extended to 90 days.

During this period, however, Ken received a letter from the Admiralty, where he was offered employment in one of their departments. This sounded like a good idea, for he was so proud of his short and near disastrous service in the Royal Navy. This would give him time to recover his former fitness, and later enable him to apply to join the Metropolitan Police, and keep up with the family tradition in that Police Force

Unaware of my brother's experiences in the Navy, my stay in Tunisia was nearing its end. We always kept our eyes open for the odd souvenir, however, particularly after the Germans had been defeated or departed. They had, to our knowledge, disposed of much of their excess weaponry by dumping items in the irrigation wells. I decided to look into that matter, and managed to put together a useful electric magnet operated by two twelve volt vehicle batteries. It worked up to a point. It was difficult getting the magnet down to the water, but bringing it up was even more difficult. The difficulty lay in getting the magnet and whatever it was holding out of the water without damaging it, or knocking off whatever we were bringing up on the side of the very rough hewn well. We overcame that by using a forked piece of tubing from the opposite side of the well, to the man engaged in lowering the magnet, to steer it past obstacles on its way back up

We picked up rifles, and other long items of metal, but these we could not always get up the side before they struck the side and came off. We picked up many smaller items but no pistols. These were what we were really after, they were the equivalent to money, because the Americans paid well for German pistols, and possession of them by British troops was frowned upon. This was a most interesting exercise, because it brought out the fact that the use of an electric magnet in such circumstances was not as easy as one would expect.

Our next move was soon upon us. We packed our vehicles and our kit, then drove to Bizerta. An interesting drive, with me hanging like a bat in my hammock in the machinery lorry. On 5th December 1943, we boarded Tank Landing Craft and sailed off to Italy.

CHAPTER 8
ITALY

To a man, I believe everyone thoroughly enjoyed the cruise to Italy. We saw Malta and Pantaleria in the distance, then passed up the side of Sicily and saw Mount Etna. The sea was flat calm, and the weather beautiful.

We arrived at Taranto late in the afternoon of 10th December, and moved inland to a staging camp. I was still getting full use out of my hammock, and occasionally trying out my meagre Italian on those attempting to sell us souvenirs. To my surprise, I found that Italian came easily to my ears, and I learnt two useful catchphrases, which explains away the major problem met when attempting to learn this fascinating language. The Italians tell you that in English you write down one thing, and say something different. Whereas in Italian, whatever you write down you say. This is certainly an interesting statement, but I am afraid, being an English speaker, I accepted the suggestion with caution, and was more inclined to accept that Italians always say what they write. I undoubtedly had a long way to go in my study of the Italian language, but was finding it most interesting and enlightening.

On 15th December 1943, we arrived at the railway station yard of Spinazola, and became heavily engaged in examining our equipment for whatever lay ahead. Quite obviously, the powers that be did not intend us to remain in this extremely pleasant location for long. With the Germans static at Casino in the face of our forces, the 1st Division were bound to be thrown in somewhere.

As expected, we were soon on the move again, firstly to Fianno, a quaint hillside village, then on to Castelamare in the bay of Naples. Almost immediately, on 24th January 1944, we boarded another Tank Landing Craft, and set sail the following morning. This was not like our very pleasant trip from Bizerta. The sea was rough, very rough, and the noise that reverberated through the ship was almost as if it was being hit by shell fire.

It was late on 27th January 1944 when we arrived at the port of Anzio, greeted by a considerable amount of shellfire, some of which passed over our heads and others thankfully falling short. We ground to a halt as we hit the beach, the bow doors opened and we all left the ship.

We followed the directions of the Military Police, up the beach and to our vehicles, which we boarded and then drove towards the flashes of gunfire that were not all that distant. After a short drive of about a half mile we parked by a large brick kiln, where we began setting up the workshop within the surrounds of the kiln. The noise of guns firing around us and shells exploding close by was almost deafening. Then there was a sound like an express train passing and an explosion over our heads followed by a truly massive explosion in Anzio town itself. Thanks to 'Anzio Archie', this was not the place for the fainthearted!

The next important thing to be attended to was sleeping accommodation. Some decided to sleep inside the shelter of the kiln, while others decided to dig themselves a dugout. I opted for the latter, and together with the Instrument Maker, 'Shalom' Gaffin, we prepared ourselves a very liveable hole in the ground covered with a quarry tipper we found.

Work in the workshop commenced almost immediately, and carried on throughout the night when necessary. My personal problem was with the guns, and the Twenty-five Pounders were giving a good account of themselves here on Anzio.

All went well until the night of 24th February,1944. Despite the noise of this location, I generally slept well with the aid of what I may have drunk in the Sergeants' Mess. In the early hours of the morning I was woken up by the sound of what I thought must have been an explosion. My friend Shalom called out to me, "Did you hear that John?" I said that I had heard nothing, but thought I had been shaken, and promptly went back to sleep.

That morning when I got up for some water to wash and shave, I noticed a large dent in the ground on one side of the dugout, and a short distance away on the town side of the dugout lay an 88mm German shell. Clearly it had landed on one side of the dugout, bounced over our heads and come to rest where found. I picked it up and took it to the nearby cliff and tossed it over the edge. Undoubtedly another of my nine lives had thankfully passed me by.

We carried on with our work, and managed to keep the guns firing regularly. It was early June before we had silenced the German artillery and bombers, much due to the massive amount of bombing organised and carried out by the American Air Force.

At the beginning of June, we were ordered to pack up and make our way north with an interesting stopover in the outskirts of Rome. We then proceeded north past Florence and on to a nice little village called Caldini.

Much of interest to me occurred whilst at Caldini. I received a letter from my father, introducing me to a former C.I.D. colleague, an AMGOT (Allied Military Government, Officer), Captain Pollock. I made contact with this man, and was invited to meet him in Rome. I went to Rome and was put up in an apartment in the centre of the city, and had a wonderful time.

I was invited to a film show for a group of very senior officers of the British, American, French and Polish armies. There had been a massacre committed by the Germans. Apparently the Italian partisans had planted a bomb, timed to go off when a German patrol met outside the military barracks in the Via Rasella. The bomb exploded, wiping out the 32-strong patrol. Herbert Kappler and S.S. Captain Erich Priebke demanded that ten local inhabitants would die for every German killed. That number of people were rounded up, taken to the Ardiatine Caves in groups, stripped of their valuables and shot. The caves were then blown in on top of these unfortunate people.

Captain Pollock had been called upon to investigate this shocking affair, and with his expertise as a former active C.I.D Officer, he truly proved his efficiency and ability. He filmed the investigation, the arrest of the man Caruso who gave the S.S. the names of those to be killed, and also the trial, and Caruso's subsequent execution. It was an experience that I will never forget, and one that confirmed my lifelong ambition to get into the Police Force as soon as the war was over.

Shortly after returning to the workshop following that memorable visit to Rome, I was fortunate in gaining promotion to Warrant Officer First Class, and took over as the Artificer Sergeant Major in charge of the Light Aid Detachment of the 19th Field Regiment, Royal Artillery. I remained in this position as the regiment moved on through Italy; then Palestine; Syria; Lebanon, and Egypt, until sent home for demobilisation.

CHAPTER 9
THE LONG ROUTE HOME

That long route home is still very much in my memory. From Geniefa on the banks of the Suez Canal, where I said a somewhat sad farewell to the men who had served me so well.

It was 26th February 1946, when I left camp for a transit camp at Sidi Bish in Alexandria. There we waited until 6th March 1946 and boarded ship for France, arriving at Toulon on the morning of 11th of that month, and to another transit camp. There we boarded a train to take us across France crowded with happy servicemen from the Army, Navy and Air Force.

The journey across France was quite long, and we were all wondering how they would feed us. We did not have to wait long to find out. We stopped at a railway station at seven the following morning. There the catering brains of the army had proof that they had solved the problem. Tins of meat and veg were simmering away in soya stoves, and we were each served with a very hot tin and a piece of bread.

The tins were served on a coke shovel, and slid off on to our mess tins. Opening them was another problem, but the contents were well worth the sometimes scalding efforts. An unusual form of feeding that went on until we arrived at Dieppe at midday on Wednesday 13th March,1946

We then boarded the happiest ship in port that day,

and steamed across the channel. The cheer that went up as the lighthouse at Beachy Head came into view said it all.

The only unusual happening on this trip followed a warning that we might all be searched on arrival at Newhaven. This was for pistols and weapons that we were not permitted to either have or bring into the country. The result was that little packages were seen to be discarded and thrown overboard by many of the returning warriors. Leaving little doubt that this exercise was repeated on every return trip bringing soldiers home from abroad, about a mile south of Beachy Head there must be a very interesting pile of rusting metal lying on the sea bed.

Once we were off loaded at Newhaven, we were issued with travel warrants to get us home, and to the demobilising centre at Aldershot. I telephoned home, and made my way to Victoria Station to be met by my parents. Words came with great difficulty, but what a joy it was to be home at last.

The following morning, I was off to Aldershot, where the speed and efficiency of the process truly amazed me. Then I proudly left the premises carrying my demob suit and a few odds and ends I had brought home with me in a card- board box. At last I was out of the army. Then a strange feeling came over me. A few minutes previously I'd been a proud Artificer Sergeant Major, a Warrant Officer First Class, a very important person by army standards. Now I was unemployed with a small job at the Co-op to perhaps go back to, but I was determined to join the Police Force before my demob leave was over.

The happy reunions at home and with friends and relatives tended to mask my inner feelings of frustration at having to wait to fulfil my one ambition to become a Police Officer. This frustration drove me to research numerous subjects that I felt might be of use to me in my intended future occupation.

CHAPTER 10
I JOIN THE MET.

My time was now fully taken up, first with sending in my application to join the Metropolitan Police, then, on 12th April 1946, with attending the recruiting office in Beak Street, Soho for a medical examination followed by yet another period of frustrating idleness and waiting.

The 3rd June 1946 was the great day. I was ordered to appear at Peel House, Regency Street, London and fitted out with a uniform. That was one point I was not happy about. After the smart turnout that I had been used to in the Army, these hastily issued uniforms seemed terribly drab. We were then sworn in by Sir Maurice Drummond, and I was for once happy and relaxed. At last, I had made it.

Twenty of us were then taken by coach to Peel House Hendon, where we were told that we were an historical class of Police recruits, In fact, the first such class to be trained at what was the Hendon Police College, originally formed for training selected Constables who would pass out as Junior Station Inspectors. Such officers were earmarked in those early days to become senior Metropolitan Police Officers and Chief Constables of Provincial Police Forces.

We were all suitably impressed. That is, until we were presented with Sergeant Duffy, our Drill Sergeant, who in addition instructed us how to stack our kit! Bearing in mind that in our class were Squadron Leaders, a Colonel,

Senior Officers in the Royal Navy, a number of Sergeant Majors from the Army like myself, and many other experienced military personnel, he did a good job. I think it took a few days before the lesson sunk in, but before we left Hendon, he became our best friend.

Lessons in law and the behaviour of Police Officers took up most of the time. These tended to be boring, but to a man we were all intent on becoming useful and efficient Police Officers, and paid strict attention to what was said. The strangest and most difficult part of this training was attempting to learn definitions and specific sections of acts of parliament parrot fashion.

How grateful we were that we were amid the fresh air of Hendon Training School, and not at Peel House in the centre of London. Here at least we could lose ourselves in the surrounding playing fields and repeat the dreaded definitions aloud, whilst walking up and down. To the uninitiated we could be thought to be crazy, wandering about and talking to ourselves, but the value of the open spaces did the trick.

It was at this point that the dreaded definition – 'The Primary Object of an Efficient Police Officer' – was brought to our attention. It was a definition produced by Sir Richard Mayne, the first Commissioner of The Metropolitan Police, in 1839, and hammered into the minds of those who wished to join this quite elite Force since those early days. Undoubtedly the words of that definition were extremely well-founded, and certainly the instructors at the Hendon Training School had no intention of permitting us to ever forget them. Throughout the course at odd times the instructor would call upon one of us in his class to stand up and repeat aloud this hallowed definition. I can assure you that, in company with many others, those words are so seared into my mind, even twenty-five years after retiring from the Force, I can still recall them vividly.

In early August, my father resigned from the Police Force. Taking into consideration his earlier service in the Dundee Police, he had completed thirty years Police service. This fact was noted by the press reporters, and various articles appeared in the newspapers. One wag had included the following quote when reporting on the imminent retirement of John Swain Senior, and referring to me as a 'chip off the old block': *'But there will still be a John Swain in London's Police Force. In a few weeks' time, his eldest son, like his father a six-footer, will have qualified to wear the uniform of a Police Constable.'* Needless to say, this brought out some light-hearted ribbing from my colleagues, but I was extremely proud to be in a position to keep the name of Swain present in the service.

That weekend I went home to Norbury, specifically for a chat with my father about the course, and perhaps pick his brains on a few points. He was as usual delighted to sit down and have a general chat. As to the course, all he could offer was that I must take in everything said, and make every possible effort to retain the information for future reference. This sounded oh so simple, but was not quite as easy as he made it sound.

Thankfully, he went on to quote a personal example. He reminded me of the letter I had written to him whilst in North Africa, about attempting to get German souvenirs out of the Arab irrigation wells by using that electric magnet. Also of the apparent frustration I had experienced in the difficulties in successfully using that magnet. He had read and re-read that letter on a number of occasions, enjoying my account and then putting the letter aside.

Then in November 1945, he had been called upon to investigate a murder on Westminster Bridge. There a Polish Air Force Warrant Officer, Tadeusz Rybcsynski, had been found shot in the chest. In his wisdom, my father decided – much against the projected cause of death, which was murder – that the man had shot himself. He was firmly of the opinion that Rybscynski had leant against the bridge and shot himself. Furthermore, that the pistol he had used must be in the Thames under the Bridge.

Then the contents of my letter had come back to him. He decided that he needed an electric magnet of such power that the currents of the Thames would not wash off whatever it picked up during the search. So he made contact with people engaged in the electronic business, with a request that they produce an electromagnet capable of picking up a pistol from the bed of the river.

Such a magnet was duly produced. The next step was to arrange with his colleagues of the Thames River Police to scour the area of the river he indicated, until they found the missing pistol. I am quite sure he must have been praying silently that his projection that this was suicide, not murder, would be proven.

He was right. A pistol bearing the registration number of the pistol officially issued to Rybczynski was recovered from the spot indicated. Furthermore, it still bore his fingerprints – proof of his use of it!

At the subsequent inquest, held at Southwark Coroners Court, the Coroner, John Walter Hulme said, "I want to say this before giving my verdict. Credit is due to Inspector Swain and his colleagues who assisted him, for the painstaking and careful enquiries they have made in this case. It is chiefly due to their obtaining the number of the deceased's revolver, and their perseverance in dragging the river until they found that revolver, that I can say that the shot was self inflicted." His verdict was 'Suicide whilst the balance of his mind was disturbed, by a shot, self inflicted.'

I came away from the most interesting meeting at home with even greater respect for my father. His final remark as I left Brockenhurst Way, Norbury that day, often comes back to me. "At the time of reading that letter from North Africa, I just chuckled and put the letter aside. It was not until I was faced with the problem of that shooting on Westminster Bridge, that the full impact of your letter came back to me." He continued by advising me to pay strict attention to the information imparted on the course. Also to remember that although you might not think it all sticks, when something important comes up at a later date, an answer to your problem just seems to appear, as it did for him in the case of the Westminster Bridge shooting.

I returned to my studies at Hendon in a most contented state of mind, vowing to attempt to retain as much as I was capable of the instruction and information passed to me. I was determined to continue to enjoy this course.

It was at this stage of the course that the instructor informed the class that we would now do a spot of play acting. The scene of an alleged accident was prepared, and each one of us was then directed to attend the scene and take particulars of what had actually taken place in our official note books.

Primed with the official opening words at such an incident – "What has happened here sir, please?" – we each waded into the apparently simple task, full of confidence. With instructors taking the part of the two parties involved, we each took down the required particulars. All nice and easy! We even carried out our respective tasks to the satisfaction of those instructors. There had to be a catch here somewhere!

The following morning the class was taken into a room that had been dressed up to look like a court room. We were reminded of the short lesson that we had been given on how to give evidence, and told that now we would find out that it is not as easy as it sounds.

To a man we were all confident that we would give a good account of ourselves. From many of my activities as a Sergeant Major in the Army, I was personally full of confidence. I knew that I could stand up in front of others and say my piece with ease.

I was in for a shock. With one of the instructors acting as the Magistrate, and another taking the part of the prisoner in the dock, I confess that I found things a little strange. There was a whole lot more to giving evidence than just reading from prepared notes in my notebook. A probing cross examination by an expert is something that has to be experienced to be understood. Most of us were quite at home standing in the witness box and saying our piece. Then the questions came, and it was quickly demonstrated to us that an expert examiner could soon induce the uninitiated to make statements quite contrary to the evidence in his notes, or given by others.

This was a most valuable experience, and one that I never forgot, for it made me realise that my evidence must always contain every truthful fact relating to the incident under review. All verbal statements must be taken down at the time, and you had to be sure that your evidence shows the date, time and place of the incident. Also when and where your notes were made.

The next shock came in the subject of observation. We were all busy studying our course notes, and the instructor was reading up on some of his work. It was a very quiet afternoon just before our final examination. Individually, each of us were asked to go to another classroom and speak to a named instructor. When my turn came, I was asked about my service in the army in Italy. We had a cosy chat about nothing in particular, except my army service. Then I was told to return to my class, and not to discuss with my colleagues what we had been talking about.

I returned to my revision in the original classroom. All was just too peaceful and quiet. Then the instructor got out of his chair and walked round the room, handing out sheets of paper to each of us without saying a word. Returning to his chair, and with something of a smug grin on his face, he calmly announced, "I want you to write down everything that you saw in that room, and no talking please." There was quite an audible groan in the classroom as he sat down and continued reading. We did exactly as bid, and each compiled a list of odds and ends seen.

Of course, another shock came when we compared a list of what actually was in that room against our own list. It seemed from our own enquiries that each of us had remembered only about a quarter of the articles actually in that room. Quite an object lesson!

We were each far from happy with our recollections of that room, but what an important demonstration of our own ineptitude. We were then reminded that during our service we would be asked to recall the contents of premises we visited on duty, and told how important accuracy of recollection was. This was a point that we all accepted and vowed to practise often.

Our course ended shortly after that all-important demonstration. We then went to Scotland Yard to have our fingerprints taken. There I was able to make a final call on my father at his office at Cannon Row Police Station. I knew he was due to leave the service at the end of the month.

As I entered his office, there was another man sitting in the armchair in his office, and my father got up and said, "What the hell are you doing here, son?" I told him I had passed the course, and would be reporting to West End Central Police Station on the Monday, but that I had come to the Yard to have my fingerprints taken. He then turned to his visitor and said, "There is no room for two of us in the job, so this is my swan song."

The gentleman got out of his chair and shook me by the hand, then turning to my father, said, "There comes a time, Jock, when we all have to leave the service" He then turned and left the office.

CHAPTER 11
WEST END CENTRAL

I commenced duty on "C" Division at Saville Row Police Station, commonly known as West End Central, on 2nd September 1946, as P.C. 272 "C". Luckily I was given a room in the nearby Trenchard House Section House, a very comfortable fourth floor room. I was told to report to the police station at 5.30 the following morning, and warned not to be late.

I made it to Saville Row Police Station on time, but with one worry. Since 1939 I had been used to having a most substantial breakfast at the start of the day. At Trenchard House, however, one could only obtain a few slices of toast and a cup of tea at 6am. Thus, by the time I arrived at the station, it felt as if my stomach was hitting my backbone. I had to solve this problem somehow, but could not find the answer.

At that Early Turn, or morning parade, I was partnered with an older Constable, Jack Warren, and told I was 'learning beats', and to listen intently to what was said. It was interesting, and certainly instructive, but boiled down to what is best referred to as plain common sense. As to my aching gut, I was told that I would soon get used to it on 'Early Turn'. I was highly relieved to find that we had a refreshment period of fifteen minutes at 10am, and I made good use of the canteen facilities at the Station. When discussing my problem with some of those who had recently joined with me, I soon found that most of them, who were also recently from the services, had suffered similarly. Between us, we vowed to do something about it. But what could we do?

We put our questions to the older Constables, and soon found that many of them were suffering from stomach disorders. They simply told us that it went with the job, and advised us to consult our doctor if the trouble continued. To me, this was too much like giving in to bureaucracy, so something had to be done.

On my second day on the beat alone, the problem solved itself. Walking along Brewer Street, I came to a cafe where the proprietor was busy getting ready for the early customers. His face was familiar, and as I turned the matter over in my mind as I slowly walked on. Then I realised it was John Walters who had been in the London Welsh Regiment with me back in 1939.

I returned to the café. John Walters was delighted to see me, and we shook hands. When demobilised from the army, he had taken over the café premises, and intended running it as his business. We spoke about our different style of service in the army, and then I mentioned my early morning eating problem in the Police. He laughed, and said, "Get yourself a small plastic sandwich box, then get a fresh sandwich and put it in the box overnight." He was aware that I was not allowed to stop and eat in his cafe, in any event he was not open before 7am. Finally he said, "Eat your sandwich, or two if necessary, with your cup of tea in the morning before you go out. Your problem will soon go." What an interesting and instructive meeting!

I found general beat work always interesting. As the Officer on a beat, you get to know those living or doing business in the area you patrol. You soon learn who you can trust, and those best kept at a distance.

I was extremely fortunate to have been posted to West End Central, covering the sleaze of Soho and the luxuries of Mayfair. Here, no Officer had a beat that he could call his own. We alternated between beats, but it was quite obvious to me that the Officer on the beat was respected by all. Yes, even the doubtful cases who you felt could even be engaged in some form of felony or misdemeanour.

Just as Soho had its own fascination of sleazy clubs, prostitutes and street corner spivs, Mayfair projected itself as the height of respectability. It had an aura of grand hotels, large houses and clubs attended by clients who turned up in Rolls Royces and the likes. Then in the centre was what I always looked upon as a village – Shepherds Market with Tony's Café, where I used to practise my knowledge of Italian with the owner, particularly when off duty, sampling his spaghetti.

During my many trips and telephone calls home, I was pleased to see how my brother Ken's fitness had quite obviously returned. Then I learned that in 1947, he had applied to join the Metropolitan Police. I sincerely hoped he would make it. The next news was that he had failed to pass this hurdle. I think my father was more disturbed than Ken on this point. He recalled to all how Ken had assisted him both during the war and afterwards, and how fit and strong he was in any task he took on. He told Ken that he felt that he should apply to another Police Force, and suggested that he applied to Surrey Constabulary. In due time Ken made his application to the Surrey Police but was turned down in the same manner. In his heart, of course, Ken realised that his sight was not one hundred percent, and that he was deaf in one ear. He put applying for the Police out of his mind, and continued working at the Admiralty, grateful that he had survived the trauma of the sinking of his beloved Bickerton.

I enjoyed my work on the beat, and arrested my quota of drunks and vagrants, but my ambition was still to get into the Criminal Investigation Department, where I felt sure I could do a good job. I therefore put in an application to be considered as an Aide to C.I.D., the first stepping stone to becoming an established C.I.D. Officer.

Following an interview with Bob Higgins, the Divisional Detective Inspector, I was posted to the Criminal Investigation Department on temporary attachment, as an Aide to C.I.D. There I was partnered with Ron Peters, an old Aide whose knowledge of "C" Division was accepted as being greater than anyone at West End Central. He was also a fund of knowledge of those who were on the other side of the law, or contemplating criminal activity.

His favourite haunt was Shepherds Market, where he was a close friend of Jack McHattie, who ran an antique shop there. This shop was right opposite Tony's Café, and when Ron was not engaged in close conversation with McHattie, we would sit in the cafe and watch those coming and going through the market. By this simple means, we made a number of quite useful arrests. In one such incident, Ron indicated a man who had just come out of a nearby chemists shop, and said, "That man is a housebreaker, I think he is a Maltese or Italian. Go and fetch him back here."

I left the café and followed the man. As he got to Curzon Street, I tapped him on the shoulder, told him I was a Police Officer, that my colleague wanted to speak to him and led him back into the market area, where the bold Ron Peters was waiting outside Tony's Café. His first words were, "I know you Mr Mora. You are under arrest. I also know that you are wanted for housebreaking in West London. You are coming with us to the Station." He then cautioned him.

At West End Central, we lodged Mora in a cell to await the arrival of Officers from Hammersmith who would be coming to collect him. I then followed my partner to the canteen. I was somewhat mystified by his surprise action in Shepherd Market. I felt that if he knew all the facts at the outset, he should have come along with me to pick up Mora, instead of sending me off like a sheepdog to collect him.

Ron just laughed. Then when he had settled down, he told me that when he had first seen Mora, he could not remember his name. This puzzled him, and while he was thinking about it, the name came back to him. So he asked Tony if he could use his telephone. He then contacted Scotland Yard, and learned Mora was in fact wanted. This was just an example of how important it is to remember the names and other particulars of villains that come into your hands, for future use.

Shortly after this unusual incident, Ron Peters took another Aide under his wing, and Bert McGowan and I, who had been on the beat together, were partnered. We worked together until October 1948, and had many interesting arrests, to the effect that we were both put forward to appear before the C.I.D. Board that month, and were both successfully accepted into the Criminal Investigation Department. The subsequent result was that in November 1948, I was posted to serve at Gerald Road Police Station in Belgravia, and Bert McGowan was posted to the Criminal Record Office.

For me, this was an interesting posting, serving on a ground where many high profile people lived. Even General Sir Gerald Templer, my old Divisional Commander from my days on Anzio during the war, lived there. As to the work, it was interesting, but lacked the inner feeling of excitement I had experienced at West End Central. The trouble was that whilst there, I had been out on the street most of the time, searching for criminals. At Gerald Road, however, I recorded allegations of crime, and followed the entry up by attempting to trace the culprit – a somewhat clerical existence. I was learning a lot about administration, which could or should stand me in good stead in future years, but was beginning to find life somewhat boring.

Then my Guardian Angel, if I ever had one, came to the rescue. I was ordered to report to Superintendent Hatherill at New Scotland Yard at ten o'clock the following morning.

CHAPTER 12
CENTRAL OFFICE, NEW SCOTLAND YARD

I asked my Detective Inspector, 'Nosher' Hearn, who gave me the order, what this was all about. He could not assist further than saying, "I don't know what Monkey Business you have been up to in your spare time, so just don't admit anything." I was the therefore even more worried. On the other hand, I knew in my heart I could not have done anything that could bring the wrath of the Yard down on my shoulders.

I duly attended the Yard in my best Old Bailey suit – black jacket and vest and striped trousers, with an Anthony Eden Trilby. For the uninitiated, this at that time was the accepted 'best dress' of all C.I.D. Officers. Bill Tennant, the Chief Clerk at Central Office, greeted me like a long lost friend, and marched me in to Superintendent Central, George Hatherill.

I had no idea what to expect. There, sitting behind his desk puffing away at a cigarette he had just lighted, was the giant of a man, George Hatherill. "So you can write shorthand lad, it that so?" I told him I could, but had not had much practice lately. "Right," he said, "take this" – notebook and pencil – "over to that chair, and take this down." Then, at a reasonable pace, he dictated a report that later covered two pages of single spaced type. On completion he said, "Now go to Sergeant Tennant, get a report form and type out that lot. Then bring it back to me."

I did exactly as asked, and spent almost all of the morning typing out this report. Oh yes, I did take my time, and was finally satisfied that it would pass muster. I handed it over to Mr Hatherill with some trepidation. He took it from me, and started reading through it, with me standing in front of him silently praying that all was well. He then put it down on his desk and sat back looking out of the window of his office. I felt that I was getting some sort of psychological treatment, and did a little more praying.

Suddenly he pressed a buzzer, and I heard the door behind me open, then Sergeant Tennant was there. Picking up the report, he handed it to the Sergeant, and said, "John here will be starting with you in the office from tomorrow." Then, turning to me, he said, "Get your gear out of Gerald Road. You now work for Central Office." I carried out this order, happy in the thought that I had impressed a very senior officer with my latent ability, and intending to continue to do so.

I duly reported to Sergeant Tennant at 9am on 20th May 1949. I had a desk of my own and commenced learning just what I had got myself involved in. They undoubtedly needed a shorthand writer but quite frankly, I was beginning to wonder why they did not use the girls from the typing pool for normal Police reports, and said so.

As interesting as the work was, I began to think – and that is not always a good thing. I could use my shorthand during an investigation, yes, but typing normal reports was a waste of my time which the Police were paying for. After all, I had joined the Police Force to become a detective, not a clerk!

I was happy I had landed the one job that half the

C.I.D. officers in the service would give their eye teeth for. The trouble was that, under this feeling, simmered my long-held ambition to follow my father and become a successful detective like him. If I remained in this so-called cushy number as an office boy-cum-clerk, for the rest of my service, I would perhaps ultimately retire as a Detective Sergeant Clerk. I wanted to work, and work hard. I wanted to be a detective.

So I carried on with my work as a very deep-thinking clerk. When I felt the time was right, I was going to put my case to George Hatherill. I could not imagine how he would take it, because he was such a serious individual. He rarely smiled, and I had never heard him laugh.

Finally, when I had to take a report in for him to pass, I took the bull by the horns. Brim full of anything but confidence, I said, " I am sorry, guvnor, but I joined the Police Force to become a detective like my father, not a clerk." I got no further. He put up his hand and said, "That's enough. If you want to be a detective, you shall have your chance."

I have no idea what was said after that by either of us. All I remember was that his upheld hand that had stopped me from continuing what I had to say, just waved me out of his office. As I returned to my desk, I heard the buzzer go, and Sergeant Tennant walked into Mr Hatherill's office. On his return, he said something like, "I don't know what you have been up to, John, but you have to report to Bob Fabian, so get your stuff out of my office now, and good luck, John, you'll need it."

June 1949 is marked in my mind by my first introduction to the man who, to everyone in the world of crime writing and investigation, was the master detective. His run of successes in solving the most difficult of cases went back many years. I knew from my past experience in the West End that his name was mentioned with both awe and respect by those on the other side of the fence as well as by my Police colleagues.

I entered his office with some trepidation, to be greeted courteously, and almost like an equal. He shook my hand and truly welcomed me to his squad, at the same time warning me that the work was not easy, and that he only wanted the best from anyone working with him. He ended up by saying, "You will be working *with* me, not *for* me. Any decision you make has to be my decision as well. Remember that." His personality projected an aura of respect in an unusual manner, for in addition it projected his respect for me – the one he was interviewing – and I found this most pleasing and unusual.

Finally I was told to contact his clerk, Ken 'Knocker' White, on the fourth floor, and settle in to a desk. Work, he assured me, would soon come my way, and it would include everything from doing 'London End' enquiries for anyone away in the provinces, to vetting applicants for important Ministry work, and investigating War Damage frauds.

Ken White welcomed me to 'The Snake Pit,' the name applied to the Detective Constables' room. There were about 15 of us there, each attached to one of the Detective Superintendents' squads. It was a happy office, as we were all loyal to our respective boss, and never discussed whatever job of work we were engaged on. The officers who were in the office on my arrival were all busy either typing out or writing up reports for the particular job they that they were engaged on. Little was said, and I, the new boy with nothing to do, began to wonder just when I would receive a call.

Ken White came to the rescue. "According to our records, you are not even an authorised driver," he said.

"I can drive, but I have not been put forward for a test as an authorised driver," I replied.

"Bloody funny!" he replied. "So how did you get posted up here? Every one of us must be able to drive a Police vehicle."

The next thing I knew was that I was taken up to Hendon Police Driving School, and handed over to a Driving Instructor. This was a rather surly individual, and we did not start off too well. "I am assured you can drive," he said, "but what vehicles have you driven?" he asked.

"Everything from a Diamond T, or a Scamell, to a Jeep or motor cycle," I replied. Clearly he did not like my reply. "Don't take the piss, son. You were an army driver, and we do not trust them."

"I can understand that, Sergeant," I said, "but I am here for a test which I know I can pass and satisfy you. My army experience is quite extensive."

We walked over to a Wolseley Police car, and on the way I was thinking to myself that even though this Driving Instructor had been somewhat surly, I had not helped matters by my attitude towards him.

He opened the door for me to get into the driving seat, then got in beside me. We then drove off along Aerodrome Road, and I followed his directions as they came to me: left turns, right turns, three-point turns in a side road, and emergency stops. Then, to my surprise, he told me to take him back to the school. As I pulled up, I said to him, "I have only asked for authorisation as a Police driver of Police cars. I have no ambition to be a Class-One driver. I just hope I have not been too cautious on this drive?"

"Yes, you are a bit cautious, but you are what we call 'safe hands', and my report will show that."

On the drive back to the Yard, my colleague indicated that too many officers expect to be classified as a Class-One driver, and the Instructors are always ready to put them in their place. Anyone who they think is seeking such a qualification is soon told that it is only given to drivers who are involved in driving up at the sharp end, like Flying Squad drivers.

On my return to the Yard, I was told that Detective Sergeant Joe Chamberlain wanted to see me. I went to his office, where he handed me a file of papers, and said, "I want you to take me to Shepherds Bush. Book out a car, and I will see you downstairs." Word certainly seemed to travel fast here – I was wanted for driving already!

From the Divisional Office, I collected a log book and keys to a Hillman Minx motor car. I went to the car that was in the yard below, got in, started it up, and waited. I was joined by the Sergeant about five minutes later. He got in and said, "Bromyard Avenue, do you know it?" I told him I did not know it, but I had an A to Z London pocket atlas in my briefcase, and could soon look it up. He assured me that was not necessary, but that I should remember the route because I would be called upon on numerous occasions to go to the government building there, as it was the headquarters of the War Damage Commission, and we in Central were always working on War Damage Frauds.

Continuing straight on from Shepherds Bush, we soon came upon a large bleak looking building that just had to be a government building of some sort. I stopped in the parking area, and the Sergeant said to me, "While I am in there, read that file I gave you. I expect I will be about a half hour." He then left the car and walked into the building.

I opened up the file. It contained a lot of handwritten papers held together with tags referred to as Foreign Office tags. The writing was surprisingly very readable, and dealt with the Sergeant's inspection of a house in Kensington. A bomb had apparently been dropped on the house immediately behind the one the papers referred to. That explosion had caused a fracture of the damp course of his house, which had necessitated under-pinning. The part referring to the underpinning was underlined in red.

The Sergeant did not return for nearly an hour. Getting into the vehicle, he asked me what I thought about the file. I told him that it looked quite straightforward, but before I offered a full opinion, I would need to examine the report to see what it was all about. I also said that it looked as if a great deal of expensive building work had been carried out.

The Sergeant was pleased that I had read what I had into his notes on this investigation, and went on to tell me that Police were only called in when there was a suspicion of fraud on the completion of the War Damage work. Also that War Damage is first of all inspected by a competent War Damage Assessor, who prepares an estimate of what has to be done, and gives an idea of what that work should cost.

In this particular case, the work involved interior plastering and painting, as well as replacement of window frames etc. The assessor had given an estimate of £1,500 for the work, whilst the bill received asked for £4,500. There had been no mention in the original assessor's report of the underpinning necessary. Therefore, it would seem that the original assessor could be at fault. As far as Joe Chamberlain was concerned, he had carried out his investigation, and had brought to the notice of the War Damage Commission the fact that it would appear that the underpinning was necessary. Whether or not the contractor should have carried out the work without first contacting the authorities was something that would be dealt with by a civil court.

Following this strange and unusual meeting with War Damage Fraud investigation, I was a regular visitor to Bromyard Avenue, usually collecting or delivering papers on this subject. I found this type of enquiry both interesting and satisfying; in fact, I learned much about building and the building trade that I was able to put to personal use later in life.

It was at about this time in my service that I had collected together all of my odds and ends of fishing tackle, a move prompted by my joining the quite elite Crystal Palace Angling Club. I found it so restful, getting away from the telephone and the demands of my superiors. Don't get me wrong, I loved my work and gave it my all. However, there were times when I just felt I deserved a rest, and an hour of quiet angling meditation with my pipe.

My son Christopher, who was then about six years old, was beginning to take an interest in fishing. Young as he was, and remembering the thrill of my first visit to Teddington with my father when I was about his age, I decided to take him to Crystal Palace lake one morning to see how he took to sitting still for a lot longer than he was normally used to. In making this decision I was awakening thoughts of my own childhood days, the frequent absences of my father, and how he had enjoyed taking me on fishing trips. As I prepared to take him with me I had a very distinct feeling that young Chris had the makings of a real good mate as time progressed. Additionally, I was quite sure that I was far more excited than he could have been.

On arrival at the lake, I sat him on a seat next to me, and explained my actions. From unpacking the rod, threading the line through the rod rings, attaching the cast and bait, then casting out. I could not say that he took in everything I had said; he was obviously interested in the ducks on the lake, and what other anglers were doing. Nevertheless, I felt reasonably sure that he had taken in some of it.

After I had caught two small bream and put them back, he questioned why I should do that. An interesting point, and just the sort of question only a child with interest would ask. I therefore gave a running commentary of my subsequent actions to which he paid obvious attention. He even asked if he could hold my rod. This enthusiasm was pleasing indeed. I cast the line a little way out, and handed the rod to him. I then instructed him how to strike, and lift the rod tip sharply when the float went down.

He showed an obvious interest in what I said, so I sat back and relaxed. At the time I was still smoking my beloved pipe, and after going through the ritual of filling it and tamping it down, I had reached the important part of the operation, lighting up. I turned into the wind, away from Chris. Suddenly he let out a terrific yell of "I've got one! I've got one!" I turned and saw my rod raised to the sky and a small roach hurtling upwards.

The fish, the line and the float were high up in a Hawthorne tree above us, and the cries of "I've got one!" continued. We recovered the fish, unhooked it, and set it free to tell its watery friends of the 'air' raising incident when it had landed in a tree. No doubt it would be some time before this fish was hooked again. Of one thing I was quite sure: Christopher was well and truly hooked on fishing and that augured well for the future.

The time soon came round when I was called upon to attend the Detective Training School on a course. I was pleased about this, because, although much of what I had learned on my initial training and since was still with me, I also knew in my heart that I would need to learn much more in order to be an efficient detective. Additionally, Bob Fabian, and George Chestney, the Chief Inspector, were always telling me that I must 'get down to the book', their favourite catchphrase. They were right, of course, and as far as I was concerned, I just wanted to satisfy myself, and learn the answers to the many small points of law that I had been obliged to ask others about.

I settled down to the course well. Our instructors were all detectives of vast experience in the field of criminal investigation. To my surprise, these officers, welcomed, indeed canvassed and encouraged us to ask questions pertaining to the subjects under review at the time. In our enthusiasm we class-members at times even asked questions that necessitated the instructor consulting one of his many books on law. To our surprise, we were encouraged to continue to ask questions, and the fact that a difficulty did arise proved to both the instructor and us that we must make every effort to memorise such difficulties for the future. Such an interesting course.

Returning from that course in 1950, I was due to sit the Sergeants' Examination later in the year. I therefore set to studying everything that had passed through my mind on the course and in the office. I had so much to learn.

Even if I passed the Sergeants' Examination, I could not really relax, as there were other examinations I had to study for. If I were to make a success of the Department, I would have to hold a First Class Civil Service Certificate of Education, and nobody knew better than I that I needed some proof of education.

Over the next two years, I became totally involved in investigating War Damage Frauds. This was a strange branch of the world of investigators. It required of the investigator common sense, a keen eye, and perseverance, combined with a vow never to be side-tracked by the builder involved, his surveyor, or the client. I was learning fast following that first introduction with Joe Chamberlain. In that case there had been some criticism of the War Damage Surveyor who had not noted that serious work, or even under-pinning, would be required. In fact my Sergeant was even complimented because he had brought to notice the damage to the property behind the one subject to the enquiry.

In October 1950, I sat the Sergeants' exam after serious concentrated study. It was a difficult paper but, to my surprise, I passed. October was indeed a very good month for me, as I also passed the First Class Civil Service Examination, without which I would not be eligible for promotion.

Late in 1950, Detective Inspector Harry Stuttard asked me to drive him to Notting Hill Gate Police Station. In Notting Hill, we arrested Jasper Martin Coetzee, who was wanted in South Africa for attempted murder. Coetzee, a former South African Air Force Pilot, was extremely pleasant, and it seemed to me at that first meeting that he was a most unlikely person to have committed or attempted to commit such a serious offence. In saying that to myself, however, I appreciated of course that this was a man wanted for attempted murder, and murderers can hardly be accepted as nice people on first sight.

Pleasant he certainly was, and his attitude towards us was that of a perfect gentleman. In view of this and the nature of the charge against him, however, we probably watched him far closer than usual. Notwithstanding this, the pleasantries continued right up to the time we parted company. Even then, he shook hands with us and thanked us for treating him fairly. That of itself was quite surprising, for we had treated him no different from others who had passed through our hands.

Extradition proceedings are lengthy and time-consuming, but at the same time they are extremely thorough. In this case, after the first hearing at Bow Street Magistrates Court, we deposited Coetzee at Brixton Prison, Thereafter, we used to collect him from Brixton Prison each week and take him to Bow Street Magistrates Court whilst the extradition proceedings were moving forward.

I listened intently to these proceedings as they unfolded, revealing the story of a domestic upheaval which had resulted in the husband, Coetzee, deciding, for reasons known only to himself, to dispose of his wife. To start with, there was an apparent message of goodwill, sent in what seemed like an attempt to heal the rift between them. He sent her a present that she had always wanted, a beautiful sewing box – one of those most useful items that opens up with trays for cottons and buttons etc.

The only trouble was that this lovely sewing box was loaded with explosives, and would have demolished the dwelling to which it was sent when opened. That is, of course, if the person who put it together – Coetzee – had really known what he was doing. He did not, and the sewing box did not explode.

Undoubtedly as a result of the wife discovering this sinister attempt on her life, she decided to move in with her mother. Coetzee, on the other hand, was aware of all the movements of the family. He had messed up the first attempt, and decided upon another ploy which was meant to indicate that he wished to put the marriage back on an even keel. Or was it to end it for ever?

Flowers. Yes. All women love flowers. This time he would make the delivery himself. He purchased a large bunch of flowers and put them together with meaning – a meaning with a difference, for the apparently peaceful and lovely offering concealed an explosive charge, triggered to go off shortly after it was delivered.

In due course, Coetzee took the flowers to the address where his wife was staying – Bethlehem, of all places (though it was Bethlehem in South Africa, not Palestine). The door was opened by his wife's mother, who would not let him into the house. She accepted the flowers, then, remembering what had happened when the sewing box had been examined, took them to the bathroom and threw them into the bath. As she was doing this, the flowers exploded and blew off part of her right hand. Realising now that he was in a lot of trouble, Coetzee made his way to Rome, and thence to London, where he was arrested.

Towards the end of the extradition proceedings, which involved my weekly attendance at Bow Street Magistrates Court to extend the provisional extradition warrant, Piet Bosman, a Detective Sergeant from the Durban Police, came to London to collect Coetzee and escort him back to South Africa. Finally, when the proceedings were over,

I took Piet Bosman and Coetzee to the London Docks, where they boarded the S.S.Goodhope Castle.

This of itself was an interesting experience. Once on board ship, the Captain took us to the bridge and, indicating the Officers' quarters, he said to Coetzee, "If you behave yourself you will eat and sleep here." Then turning round, he pointed to the open hold which contained a lot of cattle. "If you don't," he said with a frightening degree of menace, "you will eat and sleep down there." I think we were all, including Coetzee, suitably impressed. I then left the ship which sailed within an hour of my leaving.

The next thing I heard of this case was a short while later. Whilst being taken by train from Durban, Coetzee escaped from his escort and jumped from the train. The incident took place as the train was nearing the town of Bethlehem, where not all that long ago, he had delivered his explosive gifts. He was later caught and dealt with, but I heard no more about this case.

Working with Harry Stuttard on the Coetzee case brought home to me how very important it was to have what is fondly referred to as 'local knowledge'. Harry seemed to be able to just pick up the telephone and speak to a trusted contact in almost every part of London. Furthermore, I am quite convinced that following the fine example he set me as a young detective contributed largely to the many successes I had in my subsequent Police career.

In 1951, I became regularly involved in work with Chief Inspector Harry Stuttard. He had been in charge of the legendary Ghost Squad some while earlier, and his knowledge of London and the underworld was very interesting. I think it was my own interest in the East End of London, having been born there myself, that drew us together.

On one occasion we entered the Old Queens Head public house in Fieldgate Street, about a hundred yards from where I was born. Harry obviously knew the licensee, George, quite well, and we spoke together at the bar. After about a quarter of an hour, Harry said to George, "I am sorry but that character over there is wanted for robbery. I don't want to start a fuss, but that is up to him. Sorry George."

George looked somewhat disappointed and said, "If it's got to be it has got to be", and went over to serve another customer. Harry told me to stay at the bar, and to follow him out of the pub when he left with the man in question. I watched as he went up to him. They spoke briefly, then both calmly walked out of the bar like two friends. This was done in such a quiet, controlled manner that nobody would have realised an arrest had been made in the bar in their presence.

I followed, and found them both talking together beside our Hillman Minx, parked a few yards from the pub. I opened the car door, and Harry and the man got into the rear seats. I got in, started the car, and was told to go to Bethnal Green Police Station. There was no further conversation, and on arrival at Bethnal Green I stopped outside the police station and my passengers got out. I then followed them into the station, where in the charge room, my boss handed his prisoner over to the Station Officer, saying, "Your Officers want him, so now he is yours." He then sat down at the table in the charge room and wrote his report in a large book that was produced for him. After bidding the Station Officer a cheery goodbye, we left.

To me this was an experience that needed some explaining. The prisoner looked quite a tough individual. He was wanted for a crime of violence. He was found in a public house that was well known for encouraging criminals to use it. Yet my boss, a man of probably fifty, had calmly gone over to him, and without touching him, talked him out of the bar and into the street. He had not touched the prisoner, symbolic of an arrest, and there had been no offer of violence

We both left the station and got into the Hillman. "Where to, Gunvor?" I asked.

"Back to the Queens Head," came the reply.

I somehow had to start a conversation on this matter, so said, "They don't teach that style of arrest at the Training School,Guvnor."

"It would be quite criminally stupid if they did," came the reply. "I can tell you now, John, if I had gone over to that man and tapped him on the shoulder and said anything, he would have floored me before he had realised it was me he had hit." He told me that he had known the man for about 20 years, and had previously arrested him. Furthermore, Harry was well known within the criminal fraternity for being fair with the prisoners he arrested, and that counts for a lot. The first thing you have got to learn is to respect your prisoners, and show them respect. They in turn will respect you. Many of the officers who are assaulted earn the assault by treating their prisoner like a dog. "Finally, young John," he continued, "I am not asking you to become familiar with your prisoner. Without considerable care, familiarity can lead to corruption, but respecting your adversary is honourable, and to be encouraged."

With all of my examinations behind me, I still found

myself very much in the learning zone. On our way back to the Queens Head, Harry Stuttard advised me: "Always remember what you were taught at the training school. Follow those directions to the letter, and you will never go wrong. As you progress through the service, however, you will discover psychological short-cuts, like the unusual arrest you just witnessed." He then urged me to make a study of criminal attitudes, and to try to remember the attitude of each prisoner who passed through my hands. Harry Stuttard had a reputation in the Police of being a hard man. Undoubtedly, however, there was honour and gentleness beneath that apparently hard exterior.

George greeted us both with a pint at The Old Queens head. As he handed the drinks over, he said, "Thanks, Harry, for the way you took him out of the house. There was quite a conference after you had left. Everyone expected a punch up, and were surprised that it went off so well." Turning to me he said, "I don't know you, John, but if you are a friend of Harry Stuttart, and that is quite an honour, you are always welcome to come here for a drink."

Following this serious period of study and sitting examinations, I found myself committed to work in the office of the Obscene Publications Squad. I became involved with a very busy bunch of Officers under Inspector Tommy Stinton, Sergeants Bill Heddon, a former wartime army Colonel, and Arthur Stallard, and Detective Constable Jock Watson.

The work in this section for the most part came in the first instance from the office of our legal department. It was most interesting in that we worked directly with the legal eagle appointed to deal with the matter at any subsequent court hearing. However, the trouble with this type of work was that it was very repetitive. A suspect publication would be brought to our attention, and we would seek out a copy and purchase it. We would then read it, and mark out any suspect passages. The test for publishing an obscene libel was then 'whether the writing tended to corrupt or deprave the minds of those into whose hands it was likely to fall, or whose minds are open to such evil influences.' We would then send a short report to our legal adviser together with the marked copy, for his information and consideration. Thereafter, subject to his decision, we would usually be asked to seize all copies of the offending literature and prosecute the publishers. Also to obtain a destruction orders in relation to the property seized.

I found this work boring and rarely satisfying, and made my feelings known to 'the powers that be.' I was returned to 'the Snake Pit' and resumed work on the many varied types of job that came my way.

On one such occasion, I was in Lisle Street, Soho, noting the activities of builders in a particular building that was the subject of enquiry. Having recorded all that was necessary, I made my was to the nearby White Bear public house. This house was occupied by the son of a friend of my father. I fancied a pint, so walked into the saloon bar.

I had quite a shock. Arthur Richard Thurbon, a man wanted for housebreaking, whose picture was regularly in the Police Gazette, stood drinking at the bar. He saw me, but his eyes were fixed on the other bar door. This was reminiscent of the time when I used to patrol the West End with Bert McGowan. In those days, we never walked in, or entered premises together. We even used to patrol on opposite sides of the road. That action had clearly become known to the criminal fraternity, as demonstrated here. Although Thurbon's presence was no physical threat to me, I decided to adopted Harry Stuttard's approach. I made my way quietly to his side, and equally quietly told him that I was going to take him in when he had finished his drink. He said something like, "That's nice of you", drank up and walked out of the bar with me.

I walked him to West End Central Police Station, where he was detained to await an escort from the Officers who had circulated him as wanted. Thurbon was wanted for housebreaking by artifice, an unusual crime, and I decided to look into it out of personal interest. His ploy had been to pose as a War Damage Inspector. He would virtually patrol areas he was familiar with, noting the condition of war damaged premises. Then he would watch them to ascertain that the occupiers were middle aged or aged, with the man probably away from the house during the day, at work or elsewhere.

He would then go to the selected house and tell the person who answered the door that he was a War Damage Inspector, and could do something about the obvious damage. He was always received with pleasure. If an inspector had already got the matter in hand, he would put the blame on bureaucracy. Thurbon would first spend time at ground floor level, in truth looking for something useful to steal. Then he would go to the first floor with the occupier. There he would tell the person that the flooring was suspect, and would have to be attended to. At this point he would get a broom and tap on the floor with the handle. He would then hand the broom to the occupier, and tell him or her to tap on the floor until told to stop, while he went below to examine the probable damage to the ceiling He would then go to the ground floor level, steal whatever he fancied, and would be some distance from the house before the unfortunate occupier, still tapping on the floor, realised that he or she had been duped. This was a particularly heartless type of crime, generally committed against ageing victims of war damage.

Shortly after Thurbon's arrest, I was sent for by Ronald Howe, the then Assistant Commissioner of Crime, and complimented in a very sincere manner for carrying out the arrest. I felt very proud indeed, and even told him that I enjoyed working in the street, as opposed to being confined to a virtual office routine. He said nothing further than to shake my hand and mention that he would be watching my progress in the service.

As I returned to my office, I began to wonder whether I had been wise to say what I had about working in the street. I continued turning this over in my mind, then let it go and continued with my work on war damage.

Yet another surprise came when I was summoned to the office of Detective Chief Superintendent Bob Stevens, the Commander of the Metropolitan & City Police Fraud Squad. It had been decided that I was the sort of person they needed in that department. I was to hand over whatever work I had in hand to my Chief Inspector, and commence work in his department immediately. Things were certainly happening fast for me now.

Fraud Squad work can only be described as truly hard work. Not physical, but requiring a brand of concentration that tends to cloud your thoughts. Before you have solved one part of a problem, two or three similar problems arise around the same matter. To me the work was never boring. Each job was different and equally challenging. The trouble was that each job took a very large number of man hours before completion. I was not, as you may appreciate, the principal in the investigation, just the 'bag carrier' for a Chief Superintendent, or Superintendent, taking statements and administering the office needs. But my job was important in keeping the whole investigation on an even keel.

During my two years of Fraud Squad work, I was only engaged on the completion of three cases. I spent months in Wrexham, North Wales, investigating a pit prop swindle on behalf of the National Coal Board. I spent a similar period investigating the multi-letting of flats in Hamilton Terrace, West London, where ninety-nine fraudulent deposits had been taken by fraudsmen.

The third case was an investigation into 'Muck Away'. This involved the digging and preparation of the foundations of the Quinton & Kynaston Schools in the St.Johns Wood area of London. In this case, contractors had been taken on for the job of removing the excess earth from the site. The contractors, with their own vehicles usually capable of taking away five cubic yards of earth, would queue up by a mechanical digger and be loaded up. The driver would then leave the site and collect a conveyance note from the office near the site exit. The conveyance note was a valuable security, in that upon submission of these documents to the London County Council, they would be paid for their work. The Council, however, were worried that they were paying far more for their work than had ever been estimated. So the papers were passed to the Fraud Squad to investigate. The Council report was brief and to the point, and accompanied by boxes of these conveyance notes.

This was a time when the Fraud Squad was in its infancy. We did not even have an adding machine, and computers were a thing of the future. Sorting the conveyance notes was my job, while the boss, Detective Superintendent Shelley Symes, gave the orders, and kept up contact with the Council and others. I sorted hundreds of conveyance notes, by vehicle and driver, and soon found a picture that needed explaining.

(1) Adding up the amount of earth removed, it appeared that not only could the foundations have been dug out, but a pit large enough for the school or the best part of it could have been placed in it.

2) The tipping points were quite nearby, and by selecting one driver that had been paid for many conveyance notes, he would have had to travel in the region of eighty miles per hour to have done the work charged for.

(3) Clearly, a quite blatant fraud had been carried out under the eyes of the authorities, and our enquiries in the locality soon proved this contention to be true. With or without the aid of an associate, part of the fencing around this quite vast enclosure was opened for a particular lorry, which would drive in and again pass the exit point and collect a further conveyance note.

I remember Shelley Symes, when I placed this before him, roaring with laughter and saying, "They didn't shut the gate when the horse had bolted – they opened the bloody thing!"

Drill Sergeant John Swayne,
Scots Guard, Caterham 1918

John Swain Senior (far right) with colleagues of the Flying Squad in 1934

Divisional Detective Inspector John Swain "A" Division in his office at Cannon Row Police Station in 1946.

Gunner John Swain, London Welsh Regiment 1939.

Artificer Sergeant Major John Swain in Italy 1943.

Able Seaman Kenneth Swain, HMS Bickerton 1944.

Police Constable Christopher Swain, City of London Police 1996.

First class of Police Recruits Hendon Training School 1946. Police Constable John Swain back row, extreme right.

Detective Superintendent John Swain, Robbery Squad 1976.

Woman Police Constable Samantha Barber (nee Swain) joins the Metropolitan Police in 1993.

John Swain a bemedalled old Soldier visits Anzio in 1998.

CHAPTER 13
MY PERSONAL BUILDING PROJECT

Having got this far and learned so much about the building trade, and also being anxious to own my own home, I decided to take the plunge and build my own house. This was a decision that arose when considering how much I had learned by successfully investigating building fraud.

During this time, I was living in Police Married Quarters, at Sydenham in South East London, and slowly began to realise that if I remained in this very comfortable location for the rest of my service, I would find myself, on retirement, obliged to look for new accommodation. My close association with the building business also brought home to me the fact that housing prices were going up by leaps and bounds each year. My bank balance at that time did not amount to much more than a couple of hundred pounds. I had to search for accommodation that would belong to me and not the Commissioner of Police. Above all, I wanted a house with a garden similar to the one I had lived in at Norbury before the war, which my parents then still occupied.

An idea was born. I had two choices: either I would purchase a war-damaged house and do or organise its repairs myself, or I would build a house myself. To do this, I acknowledged that I would need a lot of help from someone I could trust, someone with the necessary knowledge, and who was prepared to assist me. I also realised that I did not know such a person.

Bert McGowan, who had been my partner as an Aide to CID at West End Central Police Station, was also living in Police married quarters at Beckenham in Kent. I discussed my ideas with him, and not surprisingly found his feelings were very much the same as my own. We decided to look around.

I was at the time friendly with a Captain in the local Territorial Army unit stationed at Highwood Barracks in Lordship Lane, Dulwich. He was the regimental surveyor, and a building surveyor by trade. He had given me considerable assistance and advice in some of my building fraud investigations. I mentioned my thoughts and quest to him, along the lines of: did he know of a pair of war-damaged houses that Bert McGowan and I might buy and do up for ourselves?

My friend laughed, and boldly told me that I was aiming too low. Too low! How could we afford to buy a ready-to-occupy house at current prices? But 'Jeff', as I shall call him, was not to be put off. "Buy a piece of land, and build on it," was his reply. This seemed silly to me, for I was never one to remain comfortable in debt to anyone, and I told him so. "Leave it to me," was his reply. "Í am sure I can point you in the right direction."

The matter was left at that, and I heard nothing further for some months. Then, on one of my visits to Highwood Barracks, where I occasionally gave talks to new recruits on the action of the Bofors Gun, 'Jeff' came over to me. He said he had found a plot of land that could interest me. It was in Wrights Road, South Norwood, only a few miles away, and he wanted me to go with him to look at it and consider his ideas on what could be done.

That weekend, Bert McGown and I travelled with 'Jeff' to Wrights Road. The site was truly a mess and we were not impressed. It consisted of half of the garden of a large house in Ross Road, a turning off South Norwood Hill. The actual plot itself was about two hundred feet deep and had a frontage that could easily accommodate a pair of semi-detached houses. On the site, however, were two old and very dilapidated stables.

Furthermore, the wooden fence facing Wrights Road was in a terribly broken-down condition. What on earth could I do there?

I found myself being subjected to a rather strange chuckle that my friend was well known for. It was a sound he always seemed to emit when confronted with a difficulty or problem that he could just about see through. "John," he said, "the trouble with you is that you are a detective, and I am a surveyor. I look at a site with a view to either building on it or repairing it, and I do know what is required. You only investigate something after it has happened. This, my friend, has not happened yet, but I know what is required, and I know it is something you could do." I had to listen on.

Pulling the fence to one side, the first thing that confronted me was a monstrous elm tree. I had seen it, of course, from the road, but it was not until we parted the fence that I appreciated the size of the trunk. This tree would have to be removed, but if it came down it would either fall on the stables and neighbouring houses, or into the street. There was nowhere else for it to go. Then there were those dirty dilapidated stables.

Problems there were many. The tree was just one; the cost of getting the stables demolished and the rubbish removed was something I could not even estimate. It was also work that I could not even pay for if I were to purchase this useless piece of land. "No problem," said the bold Jeff. "Firstly you demolish the stables and salvage the bricks!" As he said this, he took a penknife from his pocket and scratched away at the cement between some of the bricks. "Lime mortar," he said. "No problem, start at the top with the slates. We will use them for the damp course of the house. Clean the bricks and stack them up then use them for the footings. They are old London Stocks and very valuable bricks indeed, as bricks go." This made sense, for I had come across these very bricks in my war damage enquiries. 'Jeff' was making sense, but the task he was letting us in for seemed huge.

I expressed my feelings on the matter and asked how much they wanted for the land. The asking price was £800, but 'Jeff' felt sure he could get that price down. I mentioned Bert's and my meagre finances of Bert, only to be met again by one of 'Jeff's' stock answers. "No problem, there is a war damage claim outstanding on the stables and front fence, and if you buy the land the claim goes with it if you make it good."

I was beginning to see the light, just a glimmer, at the end of this somewhat confused tunnel. But I was still faced with the problem of having to find £400, which I did not have.

Now I am not entirely clear just how much the asking price was at the outset, or for that matter, just how much we finally managed to get the price down to. Suffice it to say that we did purchase this piece of land, thanks to the good offices of our friend 'Jeff' and, with our finances down to zero, very soon commenced work in the little spare time we had, as demolition men.

A hammer, a cold chisel, and a chopper were all the tools we required at the outset. We had the hammers and chisels, but my question was, what did we need choppers for? 'Jeff' produced some from Woolworths store, cheap choppers for chopping kindling wood. But for bricks? We were soon to learn. Removing a brick from the stable wall, he showed us how easy it was to remove lime mortar with a chopper. A bricklayer, of course, would prefer to use the tool of his trade, his trowel, but we certainly found choppers easier to handle.

The next implement 'Jeff' produced was a slating iron. I had never seen such a tool before, but it took him only a couple of minutes to explain to us and show us how this implement worked. We were learning fast, and no doubt would be adding to our knowledge as time went by.

Over the following twelve months, in our spare time before going to work when we were on late duty, and during the evenings when it was light, we slowly demolished the stables. Our combined efforts produced a large stack of London Stocks. There was also a very large heap of 'bats' – half bricks – and even a larger heap of rubble. The latter we both felt we should dispose of, but 'Jeff' would not hear of it. "You will need all of that, and probably a lot more, before you are finished" was all he wanted to say on that subject.

In addition to our labouring work, there were other equally important matters in relation to our project that had to be attended to. Even before we removed the first brick, we had to ensure that we had proper planning permission to erect two houses. We also had to employ an architect to draw up the plans, which in turn had to be accepted by the local council and building inspectors. Our greatest worry was the local Building Inspector. He turned up one afternoon when we were busy cleaning bricks. There we were, dead scruffy, dressed in jeans and overalls. He probably at first sight thought we were a pair of thieves, hence his undoubtedly hostile approach. Once assured of our honest intentions, however, he became one of our greatest allies. His knowledge of building, and his acceptance of us as we were, was to assist us over the next two years.

Our personal efforts over this painful period had produced, as I have already mentioned, heaps of useful building materials of different types. Quite frankly, we were not at all sure just what our next step would be. I use the word 'painful' because, although we had used old gloves during our brick-cleaning efforts and had worn out every pair, neither of us had any semblance of fingerprints left. This was something that proved a little embarrassing when I was called upon for elimination fingerprints after visiting the scene of a crime at a later date. The fingerprint officer immediately accused me of moonlighting in the building trade. When I explained what had happened, and my worry that my fingerprints would always look doubtful, I was assured that when I finished whatever I was doing, the prints would return to their normal state in due course.

The next problem was to get rid of the elm tree. I had ideas of cutting it down piece by piece , but it was a very large tree, and this was clearly out of the question. It undoubtedly had to come down, so we scouted around to find a Tree Feller who would do the job at the right price. Here again, our education was advanced. All artisans that we approached wanted to cut it down and take it away because the tree was useless and probably with a lot of shrapnel in it from the bomb damage. Again 'Jeff' came to our rescue. "Just cut it down and leave it where it falls, and I will tell you what to do next," was all he said.

We finally managed to find a contractor who would do as we asked. Even then, the men who did the job, which was carried out with surprising accuracy, could not understand our logic. The foreman insisted he was doing us a favour by offering to take it away, but having faith in our guide on the subject, we thanked him for the offer and turned it down. The foreman just scratched his head and looked at us as if we were mad, then turning to leave the site he said, "I'm damned if I know what you are going to do with it now. It will cost you enough to get it shifted." The very clear indication was that he was prepared to take it away for no extra charge. I had to speak to 'Jeff' again. He must have got this one wrong somewhere, but we had not proved him wrong yet.

That evening, I went over to see our guide and mentor, and explained to him what the contractor had said. He just chuckled, then there was a pause and I wondered whether he had in fact made a mistake. "I would not lead you astray John," he said. "I am in the process of selling that tree. Elm is an unusual wood, it does not rot in the sea. I am going to sell it as a pier pile, and it will end up in the Middle East.

Jeff then confessed that he already had someone who wanted to buy this tree, but first it would have to be cleaned up. Through the good offices of a friend, I was able to borrow two large felling axes. We then set about cutting off the branches, and burning them. This task took us about six weeks, and thankfully we had made friends with our neighbours, so there was no complaint about the smoke.

Then one morning, as I was enjoying a good breakfast, the telephone rang. It was a man who had seen the tree and wanted to take it away on his 'pole'. He just wanted to know when I would be there to hand it over to him. He said that he had been contracted to move it, and pay me £80 for it. I told him I would be on the site by about 7.30 on Saturday morning and probably be there all day.

As promised, I arrived in Wrights Road at 7.20 on Saturday morning. The pole was parked in the road. I had seen these weird contraptions before. There was a tractor with a small crane that pulled two sets of wheels with a long bar between them, joining them together. I then watched this peculiar looking Heath Robinson gadget haul the massive trunk to the roadside, place it on the pole between the two sets of wheels and drive off. A most impressive operation

With the site now cleared, one huge problem awaited us. We were on sloping ground and would have to dig out a platform where the houses would stand. To Jeff, however, this presented no problem, it was just one of those things that would have to be attended to and done as soon as possible. He would find a contractor who would do the job in a surprisingly short time.

Having had my experience with Shelly Symes on the London County Council 'Muck Away' job, I was very much aware of the many pitfalls in this type of work. The contractors' lorries used for this work then took away five cubic yards of earth, and were paid for the yardage of earth removed.

With money, or the shortage of it, foremost in our minds, Bert McGowan had made contact with a Building

Society who were prepared to offer us a stage by stage mortgage. First of all, however, we would have to put in the foundations, and oversite base in order to get the first payment. When we got to first floor level we would get a second grant. The third payment would be made when we got 'plate high', that is, when we had completed the vertical brickwork and were ready to put the roof on. We eagerly agreed to the terms and virtually agreed to sign over the plot of land to the Building Society, praying silently afterwards that we had done the right thing.

Now at last we were in a position to make contact with the 'Muck Away' people. This sounded easy, but there was one big problem. We would get no money until we had laid the foundations and completed the oversite. Yet we needed credit. We had little or no money, and the land upon which we were going to build now belonged to the building society who had promised to back us. Once again 'Jeff' came up with the answer.

Following his latest chuckle of satisfaction, he introduced us to contractors who would carry out the excavations required, and give us a month in which to pay. I was not very happy about this and said that we could never get to the stage when we could ask the building society for money in a month. He looked at me as if I was just plain stupid and chuckled again. "Sit down," he said, "You have got to realise that you are now in business, and business, successful business, is run on credit. So you get a bill expecting you to pay within a month. Normal procedure. You cannot pay, you have no money. Nothing new about that. So they send you a second bill, a reminder just in case the last one was lost in the post, or elsewhere. By this time, six weeks will have passed, and I will be most surprised if by that time you are not in a position to expect your first payment. Don't panic. This is business."

Our civil engineers or 'Muck Away' specialists duly arrived at the site with their bulldozers and lorries, and I was surprised just how quickly they removed the offending earth and levelled the site. The worry now was that we wanted someone firstly to mark out the foundations etc, then start to do the digging. 'Jeff', however, was in front of me on this point. He had a jobbing bricklayer, Pat Murphy, who would dig out the foundations and put in the footings after he and the architect had marked out the ground. He was a good worker between jobs, who Jeff knew well, and would wait until the oversite was completed for his full payment. After the ground had been marked out, Pat and a mate arrived to dig out the foundations and put in the first brick work. Bert and I assisted, and it was here that I realised just how unfit I had grown in recent years since leaving the army.

Whilst the digging was going on, we were reminded that we would need building materials, sand cement, and bricks. We had enough bricks for the task then in hand, but we needed a builders merchant with whom we could open an account. We were put in touch with a firm called E.R. Burt Builders Merchants of Albany Road, Walworth. We were welcomed as new customers and, on the question of credit, told we must settle our accounts by the month and within a month. That sounded all very well until the manager said that he would first have to have a look at the site.

E.R. Burt came up trumps. The manager inspected the site whilst Pat Murphy was digging away. He noted that we had plenty of bricks to hand, and agreed to supply us with sand, cement and ballast. He also indicated that although he expected to be paid within a month, as this was our first purchase and providing that we were going to purchase our building materials from his company, he would be patient until we received our first payment from the building society. My relief was such that I felt quite weak.

It was two months before we managed to get the oversite finished. The delay was due for the most part to a period of shocking weather. Then our Civil Engineers went to extreme measures to force us to pay our bill to them, and threats followed. In something of a panic, I went over to see Jeff on this problem. "Don't worry," I was told. "Civil actions in a case such as this can take quite a long while to get into the list. Certainly not less than six months. Meanwhile, your money is virtually guaranteed, you will have done your work to justify your claim for the money from the building society. They will send one of their men to inspect the ground work on the site, another delay, but only for a short time." Finally, 'Jeff' warned us not to speak with any representative seeking payment; he would write to them and explain matters.

Shortly after that we did receive a payment from the building society, and actually had money in the bank. We paid all our creditors, and built up a useful relationship with our builders merchant. As for Pat Murphy, when we paid him off, we were sorry to see him go but that was how he always worked. He would take on a bricklaying job on an expenses-only basis, to be paid in full when the job was done. He would collect all his cash in a lump sum, then go out on a king-sized binge in an attempt to drink all the public houses in south London dry.

Before Pat Murphy left us I asked him if he would continue to assist us in our project. "No," he said, "you have got to get a firm in now to finish the job." I asked him if he had any ideas of such a firm. "No," he replied, "but you had better ask 'Fingers'."

"Fingers? Who on earth is that?"

"Your mate 'Jeff', he has his fingers into all manner of people in the building trade, he is honest, and the best man to advise you."

I was not entirely happy with Pat's nickname for my friend Jeff . 'Fingers' in underworld parlance was not a word attributed to a person such as Jeff, who I knew to be a pillar of honesty and integrity. I discussed this matter with Bert, who was then stationed at Catford. Through his enquiries he located one Reg White, who ran a useful building business. We had a meeting, discussed the work and costing and were happy in our own minds as we left that Reg White could do all that we required to be done.

As we returned to the site to meet Jeff, I was turning over in my mind what he would say about us taking up with Reg White. I had nothing to worry about. Jeff was delighted, but warned us that our goal was still to get the next payment. Also, not to let the builder start on the wiring, plumbing or drains. "You do not get paid for connecting up to the sewer, although you will need a toilet on the site. Get yourself an Elsan, put up a hut in the garden, and you have your on-site toilet. The wiring can be done when you find the right man. As for the main drains, that is the last job to do."

The bricklaying went well, and it was not long before a carpenter appeared on the scene. He was an excellent worker, and it was a pleasure to see him carrying out his duties. He said little, demanded nothing, and was a superb craftsman. Therefore it was not long before I took on the job of floor-laying, cutting the tongued and grooved floorboards, and secret nailing them.

Then the bricklayers got to first floor level, and our next search was for a plumber. Nobby Clarke, who I had known for a number of years, proved ideal. He beavered away at his job and said nothing until he decided to turn on the main water to the house. Upon hearing this, the bricklayers and the carpenter put down their tools and walked into the house for a cup of tea, though not before the carpenter warned me that I should have had every joint made by 'Joker' Nobby tested before turning on the mains.

As the water started to fill up the loft water tank, Nobby could not resists shouting "Thar she blows!" The bricklayers, who by this time had reached Plate High, were not to be outdone, and remarked that they thought the joists fitted by the carpenter were too small, and would give way when the tank filled.

The carpenter, however, just smiled and focused his attention on the hallway. Then pointing in that direction, he said, "If that's not a leak, someone is not using the Elsan." We all went to that point. Sure enough, water was dripping down from under the newly installed floorboards. Nobby was the first to rush to the point, after making a feeble attempt to direct the attention elsewhere. He then let out a shout of, "I always thought you were something of a wood butcher, not a fiddler or musician, but I didn't know you could play the flute".

At first I could not see the point of this remark, which was directed at me, and clearly meant to be a joke. On closer examination, however, I fully realised what he was getting at. I was clearly the culprit. I had secret nailed a run of floor boards at an angle through one of the water pipes and into the floor joints. Nobby was relieved, and the rest of the workers were delighted that for once they could have a go at me. Therefore I bowed to Nobby's suggestion that I should buy the beer that evening after knocking off time.

The remaining work seemed to fit in like clockwork. We took on plasterers, an electrician, and even gave Reg White the main drainage work. We concreted up the driveway after hammering down literally tons of ballast and accumulated rubble.

This left one item to be removed from the site – the elm tree stump. "Dig around it and pull it out with a block and tackle," we were told. We tried this, but it did not work. Then a friend came along with a breakdown lorry, and hitched his ropes to it. All he managed to do was to make a dent in the road, and cause the neighbours' drive to lift a little.

Next we were told to bore holes in it, fill the holes with Saltpetre and burn it out. It smouldered and smouldered and stank the street out. Our final effort was made with the aid of sledge hammers and wedges, and we were still nibbling away at it after we took up occupation.

Our house was finally completed, and thankfully the stage by stage payments came in on time. We ultimately moved in on 24th December,1956. This had been a task that both Bert McGowan and I had enjoyed, despite the difficulties encountered along the way. It was a challenge from start to finish, but I doubt whether we would ever want to do it again. Certainly I would not.

CHAPTER 14
MY FIRST PROMOTION.

Happily, between us we managed to wrap up the St John's Wood job to the satisfaction of all concerned. I attended a Promotion Board, was successful, and on promotion to Second Class Detective Sergeant in August 1957, was posted to Leman Street Police Station "H" Division in the East End of London, close to where I had been born. This posting did not last long, for in October that year, I was ordered to attend Southwark Police Station in South London. There Detective Superintendent Les Wright directed me to serve at Kennington Police Station. Things were happening quite fast.

I enjoyed working at Kennington, where the local population was very similar to the people in the East End, who I had always got along well with.. My work proceeded with a modicum of success until January 1958, when I was transferred to The Flying Squad at New Scotland Yard. This was a posting I had always wanted, but had no control over how to get there. I was interviewed by Detective Superintendent Reg Spooner, who had been my boss at one time when I served at Central Office, then posted to Detective Inspector Tommy Butlers Squad, to work with Detective Sergeant Barney Gay, a former Commando, whose reputation for making good arrests was legendary.

We got along well together, but I will never forget our

first 'coffee' together. I had been formerly introduced to Barney by Tommy Butler, and now he turned to me and said, "Right, John, first stop coffee". Tom Butler laughed, and I said something like, "Sounds like a good idea" and left with Barney. I thought that we were going to Johnny's Café at Derby Gate, right outside the entrance to the Yard. Instead we got into a Squad car that was waiting in the yard, Barney said "Anchor Tap", and we moved off immediately. This fostered my first minor disagreement with the bold Barney Gay, for whereas he preferred to start the day with a pint of Courage's Best Bitter, I rarely drank until sundown. In this instance, he had his pint, and I sucked away at a half pint.

Barney and I worked well together after what may seem to have been a bad start. This was perhaps because my knowledge of London was greater than his, since I had been born in this vast city. What I truly admired about him was the number of people he knew intimately, from thieves to businessmen. Starting out one morning, Barney said to me, "Do you know Wimbledon?" I said I knew it fairly well, and asked him what he had in mind. He told me it was an area that generally projected respectability, but behind this were quite a few useful people operating there. Then, calling over to Jim Findlayson, the driver, he said, "Haydons Road, Jim."

In Haydons Road, he directed the driver to pull into Cromwell Road. There he left the vehicle, and I saw him enter a clothiers in the parade of shops on the other side of Haydons Road. He returned after about a quarter of an hour. "Cigarettes by the thousand are moving round here, John," he said. "A plain van pulls up, the driver gets out, enters the cafe, and then returns and takes out a case of something and carries it into the cafe." To back up this statement, Barney had the registration number of the van. "It arrives every day, and should be there some time this morning."

It was now a quarter to eleven. Barney gave me and the driver the number of the vehicle, then said, "We will let him do his drop, then stop the vehicle a short distance away."

At a quarter to twelve, a medium sized box van stopped outside the café, and the driver got out and entered the cafe. He returned to his vehicle, opened the back door, took out a case of something, closed the rear door, and re-entered the café with the case. He came back almost immediately, got into his vehicle and drove off south in Haydons Road.

We drove after the van and stopped it as it turned into North Road, opposite a recreation ground. The driver, Ronald Shaw, said, "What's this all about? I have done nothing wrong." We got him to open up the back of the van, but there was nothing there. Quite empty! "Very nice," said Barney. "Next stop, Wimbledon Police Station."

Having lodged Shaw at the station, we returned to the cafe. The proprietor was not very co-operative. We moved into the rear of the cafe, and found in his store a heavy cardboard case, bearing the clear impression of where a label had been cut out. He would not tell us what was in the case, so we cut it open. Sure enough, it contained cigarettes. We took the case and contents together with the café proprietor, Charles Barnes, to Wimbledon Police Station.

Shaw was brought into the charge room and, on seeing Barnes sitting there, indicated the case of cigarettes and said, "Fair dos, Guvnor, I am not going to say any more." We spent a little time on Shaw, who it seemed wanted to clear the matter up. Meanwhile, as the result of enquiries made through Property Index at the Yard, we identified the cigarettes as having been stolen by warehouse breaking in Hoxton. There, it seemed, a number of cases of cigarettes had been stolen, cases of the same dimension as the one we had taken from the café.

Shaw admitted this offence, but had no intention of telling us who he had sold the other cases to. We questioned the café proprietor Barnes, telling him that he had been seen to receive other cases from Shaw, but he would not believe us or admit further involvement than receiving the one case. In truth, we could not take the matter further. Barnes was therefore charged with receiving one case of cigarettes, knowing the same to have been stolen, and was dealt with at the local Magistrates Court.

As for Ronald Shaw, we took him to Old Street Police Station, where he was charged with warehouse breaking. Prior to charging him, we had searched his home address in Stoke Newington, but found nothing linking him to this or other offences. He was finally dealt with at the County of London Sessions, and sentenced to a term of imprisonment.

Earlier, during the enquiries into this matter, I asked Barney what his friend at the clothiers shop in Haydons Road, had to say about the matter. His reply was that he had met the manager of the shop socially, and the man had sounded as if he could make a useful informant. This had proved true, and perhaps he would turn up further useful information in the future. Barney intended to thank him for his accurate information, then to ensure that the man received a reward from the Information Fund and thereafter kept his eyes open for similar activity, for which he would also be rewarded. "That," said the bold Barney, "is the most important part of the making of an informant, and encouraging him to keep up his usefulness."

My partnership with Barney Gay proved to be the most important learning zone of my Police career as time moved on. He was such a fund of knowledge on how to treat both prisoners, informants, and the public generally. He had the traditional patience of Jobe during interrogations, and a memory for seemingly insignificant facts that was quite stunning.

Largely due to his knowledge of the London underworld, and his ability to attract and use informants without exposing them, we had a wonderful run of successes. At the time, I had purchased a useful Lambretta Motor Scooter, for the purpose of getting to work through the early morning traffic. When Barney saw my latest means of transport, he could not resist a comment. "Just the job, there is a receiver up in Islington that I have been trying to track down for some time. He knows his business, but we cannot get near him with our line of transport. We must give your scooter a trial run."

So we moved off to Islington. Our target lived in Brownlow Road, Haggerston, and during the journey it was decided that I would park my scooter in sight of the target address. There, I was to sit on the curb, take off the engine inspection panel of my machine, and watch the address, ready to follow him immediately if required.

The plan was that I had a good description of the target, Charlie Forbes, a former railway worker, suspected of being a receiver of stolen lorry loads. When he was seen to leave his home, I was to follow him. It was expected that he would make his way to a van parked somewhere in the vicinity, then go to his 'Run-In', load up with goods, then take the load to his customer. Barney would be parked up at a distance with me just in sight. When I moved off, he would attempt to follow me at a distance. Under no circumstances did he want the suspect to see the Squad Jaguar until it was decided to stop the van.

I sat on the curb apparently tinkering with my broken down scooter at 8.30am. At five to nine, Forbes came out, walked to Queensbridge Road, turned left and walked towards Hackney Road. There he stood on the corner and lit a cigarette. After five minutes he retraced his steps up Queensbridge Road and turned into Whiston Road, turned right into Dove Row, then left and left again into Whiston road. There he turned left towards Queensbridge Road, stopping by a small Ford van that he had passed earlier, opening the drivers door, and getting in. I had no idea where my colleagues were, and followed on.

We had covered this very touchy point in our earlier discussions. I was to follow the target, and Barney was to follow me at a distance. He knew that this could well prove to be difficult. From previous attempts to follow this exceptionally cunning individual, therefore I was to call the Squad office from a public telephone when in need of their assistance! Furthermore, if I wanted my colleagues to join me I would pull up and take the engine cover off and place it on top of the seat of the scooter.

Forbes drove through Hoxton to New North Road, where he stopped by a closed railway arch, opened up the gate and drove his van inside, then closing the door behind him. I could not see the Squad Jaguar, so sat on the curb fiddling with the scooter engine, having placed the engine cover in the required place. At ten thirty, Forbes emerged from his hiding place, driving his van, first locking up the arch.

I followed on, and was glad to see that my colleagues had seen me start off again. I again drove through all manner of back streets, finally arriving at Cloudesley Road, Islington. There the suspect stopped at a café and went inside. I watched until he came out and opened up the rear doors of the van.

He then took out a large square package and went back into the café with it. Looking back, I saw Barney leaning up against the wall some distance away giving me the thumbs up signal, confirming that he had seen what had taken place. The suspect then came out of the cafe, got into his van and drove off. As I was replacing my engine cover, the Jaguar roared past me. I saw it turn into Barnsbury Street, and on my arrival there Barney was standing by the van now jammed into the curb by the Jaguar.

There were four more cases in the van. The labels had all been cut out. The van was then driven by Forbes, accompanied by Barney, to Clerkenwell Police Station where he was detained. The next move was to return to the café in Cloudesley Road. There we had a quiet talk to the manager, and found the case which we had seen being taken in. It had been cut open, and some of the contents were now displayed in the café, ready for sale.

The café manager was in a co-operative state of mind, and took down those he said he had removed from the case earlier. We then took him and his property to Clerkenwell Police Station. There both Forbes and Roberts, the café manager, were charged with receiving stolen cigarettes, knowing the same to have been stolen, and subsequently dealt with by the Courts.

The following three points are the guts of the life of

any experienced investigator, and the most important matters that prove his worth: (1) Time may drag on when one is on a solitary and boring observation, or (2) sitting in the ante-room of a court waiting to be called as a witness. (3) Worse still is sitting in your office writing out the framework of a complicated legal aid report, prior to dictating it to a shorthand typist, then presenting it to the legal eagles to scan.

At this particular time of my life as a young detective, I was beginning to appreciate the work that must have gone into supervising, instructing and guiding me in my chosen profession, to the extent that I made up my mind that I too must get into the supervising side of the Police. The problem, however, was how. I could think of no way to bring that about, apart from passing the next and most difficult promotion examination. I loved Flying Squad work, but as a Squad officer, it was almost impossible to spend the necessary time studying. I was in a state of frustration that I would have to come to terms with. It was an experience I had never felt so strongly before, and one I would have to shake off.

CHAPTER 15
POSTED TO BRIXTON

On 7th December 1959, I arrived at the Yard determined to seek some advice on the subject that had plagued me during the recent weeks. On my way to the Flying Squad Office, I passed the clerk's office and a voice called out from within. John, Uncle Reg wants to see you, you had better go in there."

This sounded good to me, as I had so much I wanted to say. I knocked on the boss's door and received an invitation to 'come in'. I entered and stood to attention in front of Reg Spooner, the one boss for whom I had utter and absolute respect and admiration, and said, "Sir".

Through a cloud of smoke, he said, "Alright, John, you`re not in the army now, that's enough of that." I relaxed, he was obviously in a very good mood. His next words were, "I believe you're very happy on the Squad. Is that so?"

"Yes, sir, " I replied.

"Too bloody happy, I believe?" I was not sure how to answer that one. I was so busy trying to work out what he had on his mind. Then he said it. "Yes, too bloody happy to study. You do not realise that you are going through the most important part of your career right now. It is now that you can formulate your future. Study and pass your exams and become someone, or just soldier on as one of the lads, arresting criminals and enjoying life as it comes. Pack your kit, John. You have been posted to Brixton. There you must study, and study hard. If you get through you may have a chance to get back here, but no promises, the rest is up to you." He stood up, reached over and shook me by the hand, saying, "Good luck, John, my regards to your father. I know he will agree with me."

Barney Gay was waiting for me in the main Squad office. "What was that all about, John? What have you done wrong that I don't know about?" I told him what had taken place, and that I was now posted to Brixton. Barney was sorry to find me leaving him but insisted that the only way further up the ladder in the Police from Second Class Sergeant, was to pass the dreaded First Class Sergeants' Examination.

I sadly left the Flying Squad office and The Yard that morning, and reported to Brixton Police Station. I had already learned the basic lessons of being a lowly detective sergeant whilst briefly at Leman Street and Kennington. I was determined, somehow or other, to leave my mark at Brixton, so set to studying the crime books. There were many coloured people living in this area, and from what I read, the crime problems such as they were were either linked to them, or to the street traders mixed in with Brixton market people.

I decided to have a walk round the market area, and also Somerleyton Road and Geneva Road. My first stop was the nearby Volunteer Arms. As I walked in, a cry went up: "Swainey! What are you doing over here?" It was Freddie Jones, who I had arrested for obstruction of a uniformed Constable in the West End. I had also pulled him in for selling obscene magazines from a pavement stall when I was an Aide to CID. Freddie was always one of those who just had to be into something. Whoever his friends were, they had to be interesting. I lied to Freddie, telling him that I had been posted to Brixton for a rest after the West End, and left the public house.

From The Volunteer Arms, I walked to Somerleyton Road. This was a road used almost exclusively by coloured people. As I passed one house, the noise of chatter and raised voices came from a basement flat. I walked down the steps and entered the room. A number of coloured men were playing cards, dominoes and dice Then a loud voice from somewhere in the room called out, "Mister Swain! What are you doing over this side of the river?" It was Seaford Allen, better known as Tommy Farr, a large Jamaican who I had met when serving at Leman Street, and known there as something of a pleasant, gentle giant. He had never given trouble over there, and I hoped that his general attitude towards the Police would not change. I told him I was now working from Brixton Police Station, and would no doubt see him again in due time. It was quite reassuring to know that I had something of a friend in this unusual environment.

I soon found that my work here was mainly involved in supervision: guiding Officers who had brought charges into the station, ensuring that they had correct and positive evidence, and that they adopted the correct procedure in relation to it in their particular case. It was a style of work that was new to me, but always appreciated by the Officers concerned. Probably the most interesting man I met there was Detective Constable John Bland, and we have been good friends since those days.

It also made me realise the importance of the study I was doing in every spare moment. I recall on one occasion chuckling a little when I was walking round the area, repeating aloud a definition of a particular Act of Parliament that was giving me trouble in my study. I remembered the time I had questioned my father on this same subject, and his assurance that what I was now doing – talking aloud – was the best method of instilling the subject matter in your mind.

I enjoyed my stay at Brixton and the work that went with it. I was successful in the investigations I took on, and earned the respect of my superiors, who were ever on to me to continue my study and pass the next and most important examination of all, reminding me that if I did not pass, I would get no further promotion in the service.

I needed little more advice than that. I had no desire to remain a Second Class Detective Sergeant for the remainder of my Police career. I urgently needed to prove myself to my greatly respected father, who always took an interest in my activities in the Police.

I found study for this particular exam most difficult. There were times when the concentrated study made my thoughts numb and blank, and I just could not retain the last definition from a particular act. This all reminded me of my experience at the Military College of Science during the war, when I was studying to become an Armament Artificer. On that occasion, I had cast everything from my mind, and succeeded. I repeated that exercise this time and, in December 1962, sat the exam. Yes, I did pass muster, but it was the wait after the papers had been collected from me in the examination room that made me sweat. I knew in my mind that I had submitted a good paper. I had gone over my submission in my thoughts a hundred times. My worry was that the eagle-eyed examiners might find an error I had made, which could reduce my marks below the very high standard required.

In early February 1963, I was delighted to read in Police orders that I had passed the examination, and was posted back to the Flying Squad as a First Class Sergeant. What a relief!

CHAPTER 16
BACK TO THE FLYING SQUAD.

I have always been glad to say that, throughout my service in the Metropolitan Police, I generally felt happy and at ease. Furthermore, in all circumstances that state of mind prevailed, and I was fortunately able to adjust myself to the strange, new and sometimes difficult situations as they arose.

The 8th February 1963 was one of those strange days. It was strange in that my previous good friend and Flying Squad boss, Detective Superintendent Reg Spooner, had moved on in the job, and my former Detective Inspector, Tommy Butler, was now the man in charge, and the man I had to report to.

I had no idea of just what to expect from Tommy Butler, but was determined to carry on the good work, and project myself in a light that he would appreciate. I was greeted with a handshake and a "Glad to see you back here, John. If you don't know Detective Inspector, Fred Byers, you soon will. You are going to his team on my recommendation, so don't let me down." I assured him that I would keep up the good work, and certainly would not let him or anyone else down for that matter. He then waved me out of his office.

In the main office, I located 'Big' Fred Byers, truly a big man, with a big reputation for his vast knowledge of West London. He welcomed me to his team, and went on to tell me that he was well aware of my knowledge of South and East London, and hoped that I would soon put it to good use.

At that moment, John Bland walked into the office, and was introduced to me. "I know that you know John Bland from your service at Brixton," said the Inspector. "He is now your partner, and if what he has told me about you is true, you will soon be bringing in thieves in the same way you have done in the past down at Brixton.

John and I made our way to Brixton and did the rounds of people we both knew, spreading the word that we were working together on the Flying Squad, and would welcome any information that passed our way. We also pointed out that if the information was good, there could be a grant from the Information Fund for the informant. It was not the wasted day I had felt it could have been. We learned that nylon stockings were being offered for sale in the West Indian gambling clubs by a woman from West London named Mary Flynn. The nylons were boxed, and looked as if they had come from a shop. According to Mary Flynn, they were part of a job lot that she had obtained from a dealer in Shepherds Bush Market. Our West Indian informant, however, assured us that they were of well known brands and were offered at just under half the price of those on sale in local shops.

All we needed was a little more information about this mysterious woman, who, we were told, had just arrived without notice at one of the clubs with her wares, sold them and departed. They were a good cheap buy and were soon all sold. There had to be a useful job here somewhere, but first of all, how do we identify this woman Flynn, and where does she come from? From the quantities that we were told had been supplied by this woman, her goods were undoubtedly coming from a store, or 'Run In', where the contents of a stolen van or warehouse-breaking were being kept.

We made a round of enquiries in all of the clubs that John Bland and I knew in the Brixton area on the pretext that we were interested in drug traffickers. Thus we were able to build up a good description of Mrs Flynn without showing too much interest in her. We plied our new found informant, who we called Carl, with as much beer as he wanted, and just prior to leaving he told us that Mary had a small red Ford motor car in which she brought her goods to Brixton - all boxed nylon stockings in sacks! Furthermore, when she came she would sell all of the stockings she had, and had told one of the club owners, that when she drove home, she always drove an empty car, so that if the Police stopped her she would have nothing to worry about on board. We told Carl that just out of interest, we would give him a bottle of whisky if he could tell us the number of the vehicle. This undoubtedly pleased him and fired up his enthusiasm to assist. He said he should be able to get the number during the week, and would telephone us at the Yard when he wanted to meet us again at our agreed meeting place in Brighton Terrace.

We parted after warning him that he should not give the number to anyone else except us, and then only in person. Then, to make the job easier for him, we told him to telephone us on the next occasion the woman was doing her rounds, and then to meet us at the agreed location. We also reminded him that if he wanted to see us himself, irrespective of the type of information he had, he could just leave a message to meet Carl at whatever time was convenient to him. Also, just to leave the time of the meet and the name Carl, with no mention of where the meeting would be. We also told him that we could be anywhere in the London area, so the distance from Brixton could be considerable. Thus he might have to wait for us for some while before we arrived.

Our friend Carl was thoroughly enjoying the spirit of conspiracy and free drinks surrounding our friendship, and promised to be in touch with us in the very near future. We both felt happy that we had a man who would at least try to assist us, and we certainly needed someone who would do as they were told, and report only to us about his findings.

The following morning we reported to the Squad office at nine. Carl had left a message for us during the night to meet him at 10am. He refused to say where the meet was supposed to be, and the night duty telephone operator was somewhat upset when Carl had told him to just repeat the message to us, and to assure him that we would know when and where we should meet. John and I made our way to Brixton, parked the car well up the road, and walked down to the agreed meeting point. He was not there! Then, as we decided to wait, Carl just turned up out of the blue. Neither of us noticed him coming until he was on beside of us.

He had written the car index number on an old cigarette packet, and handed it to me. He told us the club the woman Flynn had visited, and also that the club owner would not let the stockings remain on his premise. His customers who bought them had to take them away from the club when the time came for them to leave.

Now to check the information. Our first job then was to ascertain who the vehicle was registered to, and this should not cause any difficulty, providing, of course, that she had registered it in her name and true address.

We waited for the reply to this enquiry with baited breath. Then came the reply. Yes, she had registered the vehicle in the name we knew, with an address in Sussex Gardens, Bayswater.

We moved off to Sussex Gardens. The address consisted of part of a large old Georgian house divided up into small flatlets. We then decided to cruise the area looking for the maroon Ford Prefect. We found it parked in nearby Sussex Place. I decided that we would keep observation on the house, and to be in a position to see the entrance of Sussex Place, then sat back for a quiet smoke. It was close to noon by this time, and it looked as if we could be in for a long wait, and advised the Squad office that we were engaged on an observation, and would report when there was any movement.

At 4.30 that afternoon, a woman came up from of the basement flat of the address. She looked up and down Sussex Gardens, went back down the steps and inside. Peculiar, but very interesting. It was the almost copybook action of someone who had something to hide, or was frightened of 'something'. We did not move.

Five minutes later the same woman, but wearing different outer clothing, returned from the lower flat. This time she turned right and walked to Sussex Place, got into the Ford Prefect, and drove towards us, turned left into Sussex Gardens, stopped outside her house and sounded her car horn. Up the steps trotted a man aged about 35, who got straight into the waiting motor car. The car was then driven past us, and on past Paddington Station to a lock-up or garage in Bishops Bridge Road. There they both got out of her car, opened up the lock-up, went inside.

Within a minute or so, Mary came out carrying a bundle which she put in the back of the Prefect. She then went back into the lock-up. We joined her and her partner who was standing by a small Bedford Van. "What have you got here," I asked in my most polite manner.

She just laughed and said, "I've just bought this job lot in the market, and am going to take it to my shop."

Again in my most polite manner I asked, "And where would your shop be, my dear?" I then put my hand into one of the bags she had in the car and brought out a box of nylon stockings. Her companion said nothing, so I took his name – Michael FLYNN – and particulars.

He then said, "I am a dealer and work Shepherds Bush and other markets. The gear in the van is mine to sell." I then questioned him as to where he had obtained the property. He could only say that he did not bother with receipts he had bought the Nylons from another dealer, and that he did business on a handshake! I had heard this style of talk so many times before. In my own mind I was satisfied that this property was all stolen from someone somewhere. I then told him that unless he could satisfy me that the goods had been genuinely purchased by him, we were going to take both of them to Paddington Police station whilst further enquiries were made.

"O.K.," he said, "but you are making a big mistake, and this is nothing to do with my wife Mary. Let her go please."

Having lodged the couple at Paddington Police Station, we called up the Detective Inspector and told him what we were doing. We also asked him to arrange for Jumbo's Club in Railton Road, Brixton, to be searched, believing that there could well be still some of the stockings that Mary had sold there on her visit the previous night. "Consider it done," said the bold Fred Byers. "Call me up if you need anything further."

John Bland and I then made our way to the lock-up which we had sealed before leaving with Mrs Flynn. The van had contained forty boxes of nylons. There was no paperwork that could indicate where this property had come from, and quite frankly we did not expect to be able find such information after what Michael Flynn had told us.

The Flynns were both charged with receiving a quantity of nylon stockings valued at £500, knowing the same to have been stolen. We then left Paddington to take a statement from the Brixton Club owners, who promised to assist this prosecution.

Our subsequent enquiries failed to identify just where these nylons had been stolen from. As to the Flynns, they ultimately pleaded guilty to the charge and were dealt with according to the law. We gave Carl a bottle of whisky for his trouble, and after the case had finally ended, he was granted a reward from the Information Fund. After this particular case, I met Carl on many occasions at our agreed meeting place in Brighton Terrace, with similar successes.

Meanwhile, my son Christopher had spent his spare time keeping himself exceedingly fit by taking up cycle racing, a calling no doubt prompted by the fact that I had taken up the sport myself at 17 years of age. In August 1964, shortly after completion of the Flynn job, Christopher decided in his wisdom to apply to join the City of London Police Cadets.

There, as the result of the in-depth medical examination that he was subjected to, he proved to have an excess of albumin in his urine. That examination took place the day after he had cycled back from Exeter, having spent a week in Cornwall touring on his cycle. He mentioned this to the examiner, who promptly sent him to St. Bartholomews Hospital. There he was detained as an in-patient for a few days, and finally released with a clear bill of health, after being told that his problem had undoubtedly been caused by the excess of energy he had used pumping his cycle over the many miles of his tour.

He became a City of London Police Cadet in October of that year, and thoroughly enjoyed the work involved.

My successes in late 1964 induced my bosses to recommend me for consideration to promotion to the rank of Detective Inspector. In February 1965, my promotion was confirmed, and I was placed in charge of Five Squad, the team I had joined on my first posting to the Flying Squad in 1958.

Before I had time to settle down, Commander Tommy Butler sent for me sent for me. I thought this was rather sudden and made my way to his office deep in thought. I knocked on his door and was invited in. Then, to my complete surprise I was told to take a seat. He was busy this time turning papers over on his desk. He looked up and said that there was a vacancy on my team for a Detective Sergeant, and asked if there anyone I would particularly want to bring into my squad.

This was indeed an honour, and for a moment I was lost for the right word. I then said, "Give me a pink faced young man who really wants to learn, who will do as he is told, and not argue with my decisions. Above all, I do not want a 'wide boy' who thinks he knows it all." At that point I was cut off by the Commander, who leant back in his chair and roared with laughter, something that he was certainly not known for. Then when he had settled down, he waved me out of his office, saying, "I think

I have just the man for you."

About a fortnight after that interlude, Mike McAdam joined my team. We had never met before, and I knew nothing about him. He was, however, everything I had asked for and much more. He subsequently turned out to be one of the finest detectives I have ever met. Furthermore, we are now both fully retired, and are still close friends.

Shortly after the arrival of Mike McAdam, I received somewhat vague information that there was going to be a robbery at Lloyds Bank Lombard Street, in the City of London. I knew the area well, and could not imagine any team of robbers attempting such a robbery because of the difficulties of getting away from the scene safely, in the obvious hurry after the event. We examined the scene, and to our amazement found that our Police radios would not work in the very enclosed space of this narrow and built up road.

We approached, and were most grateful to receive the full co-operation of the City of London Police. They had experienced just the same difficulty when Police Radios had first come into being, and were well ahead of the Metropolitan Police on this matter. With the aid of their more advanced equipment, we checked the area thoroughly, but could still not see how a robbery, armed or otherwise, could take place here.

With great difficulty we set up an observation on the bank commencing at 6am. Then enquiries revealed that sometime between 6am and 7am, waste paper was taken from the bank to a nearby collecting point. Then the informant came up with the suggestion that the robbery would be on a Saturday morning, the day that banks are not open for business.

We spent a number of weeks examining thoroughly all of the probable scenarios of a robbery at this very enclosed point. We only managed to confirm that waste paper was brought out some days early in the morning, shortly after 6am from the side entrance in Change Alley, off Lombard Street by two bank workers. It was then taken to a pick-up point at Post Office Court, and left there for contractors to pick up. Our observations were thereafter geared to Saturday mornings, with well pre-pared observation points pre-arranged.

On Saturday, 6th November 1965, members of my team, a detective from the City of London Police and myself were in position well before 6am. At 6.15 a man in overalls came out of the side entrance of the bank, went to some waste paper bins and returned to the bank. The same man, Richard Barton, repeated this move on four or five occasions during the next half hour. At about 6.40am, a second man in overalls, Frederick John Williams, came out of the side entrance of the bank with a sack and disappeared in the direction of King William Street. At about this time colleagues watching in King William Street, saw Dunlop, Clarke and Curtis deposit heavy sacks from a vehicle at the collecting point.

At 7.30am.Wiliams and Barton came out of the side entrance of the bank, walked to Post Office Court, There, they picked up the two sacks left by the three men previ-ously seen, who had been arrested by my colleagues and taken to Cloak Lane Police Station. It was now a matter of getting my officers together, and getting into the bank. Fortunately Williams came out of the side entrance again and went over to the bins. There I stopped him, told him we were Police Officers and took him into the bank to examine what he had just taken in. He insisted that he had only brought in waste paper. Nevertheless, we took him to the basement office where he worked.

As Williams led us down the stairs, I found that of all things, the Primary Objects were flashing through my mind! This in the haze of the search for evidence to support us for actually being inside the bank early on Saturday morning. Yes there had obviously been something heavy in one of the sacks carried in by these two men. One sack in particular had what appeared to have an oxygen bottle protruding out of the top. As Police, we were there for the prevention of crime, or the detection and punishment of offenders if crime is committed. It certainly looked as if a crime was about to be committed, and we could well prevent it happening. Then followed those wonderful words about the protection of life and property, and the preservation of public tranquillity. If we had not been there to prevent what was supposed to happen, there could have been all manner of mayhem and panic inside the premises that morning, and the tranquillity of those who were actually working in the bank could have been disturbed in a most unholy manner. Robbers usually have guns or other instruments of violence readily available.

The two men were most convincing liars, and the more they lied, the happier I was. On searching Williams, three skeleton keys were found. He insisted that they were bank keys and that he had signed for them. Barton, however, was a different type of person, and I felt that if anyone had been used, it was Barton.

The search that followed was vast, time consuming, and difficult. Then at 9.25am, after contact with the Yard, a bank official arrived at the scene. He was most upset to find us actually inside his bank, but when the skeleton keys found on Williams proved to operate in pairs, and were capable of opening every vault grill except the internal strong room grill, he became more amenable. Then after a call from Detective Sergeant Gwyn Waters, I went to a temporary storage cupboard where he had found two gas cylinders and items of cutting equipment. We then took the two men and this equipment to Cloak Lane Police Station, later to be joined by the three men Dunlop, Clarke, and Curtis, who had been arrested after they had dropped the offending articles at Post Office Court earlier. All five were charged with conspiracy to steal from Lloyds Bank Lombard Street, but the vagaries of the matter were not over yet.

We had all of the evidence readily available, even Learned Counsel were complimentary about the way it had been put together. The committal proceedings from the Mansion House Magistrates Court, went ahead without a hitch. Then at the Central Criminal Court, or Old Bailey, things started to happen!

We are proud in this country of the fact that every prisoner has the right to challenge a juror, but in this case it went a little further than the norm. A great number of jurors were challenged, certainly far more than I had ever experienced. Complications were such that two trials took place, this after one jury had been discharged and another empanelled.

Stories of jurors being approached to give a 'Not Guilty' verdict and offered bribes continued. There was irregular behaviour that honest jurors brought to our notice. Then a further application for the jury to be discharged, which the judge refused. The antics of approaching jurors went on, with the honest ones coming forward but notwithstanding all of our efforts, the jury finally found four of the accused Not Guilty, with Williams alone being found guilty and sentenced to five years' imprisonment. This all happened in the era when a unanimous verdict was obligatory upon the jury. My team and others had worked hard to encourage jurors to come forward when approached. Some had come forward, but somewhere in this jury, someone had remained silent in the face of a bribe.

Apart from myself and my team, the law officers engaged in the prosecution and the judges were most disappointed with the verdict. For my part, however, I like to think it was my efforts and those of my men that did much to prevent further jury nobbling, and bring about the change in the jury system from the once obligatory unanimous verdict to the majority verdict that is accepted today.

September 1967 held other surprises for me. My son Christopher had by now passed through the normal Cadet process, and had been sent to R.A.F. Debden in Essex on a three month Police Training Course. He passed with flying colours, but his training was not over yet. He was next required to attend an in-house training session for a period at Bishopsgate Police Station. After that he was posted to Snow Hill Police Station, and spent a month on patrol with an older Police Officer, learning the art of becoming efficient in his work as a Constable. I was happy in the knowledge that he was enjoying the challenge of being an officer of the law. I therefore vowed to leave him to his own devices, and to restrict my interest to just keeping up to date with him on a need-to-know basis.

His first patrol, alone in Fleet Street, brought out much of the need for a clear head and sound judgement in his activities. Walking from Ludgate Circus into Fleet Street, he found the road completely devoid of delivery vans. Then his attention turned towards a private car driving towards him flashing his headlights. The driver slowed down and shouted to Chris, "You had better get up there", indicating further up Fleet Street. "There's been a nasty accident, and there are people who have been very obviously hurt."

Chris made his way to the area indicated, and found that a private motor car had smashed into the back of a parked delivery van. Both the driver and passenger had passed through the windscreen of their car and had some nasty facial injuries. Chris called in an ambulance, and made arrangements for the damaged car to be taken in. He then hastened to Snow Hill Police Station to make out his report on the incident. The Breathalyser had only just been introduced, and Chris had never even seen one, but his sergeant gave him a proper roasting for not Breathalysing the driver. Chris took the telling off without commenting further, firmly believing that he had done the right thing by sending the severely injured parties off to hospital.

CHAPTER 17
PROMOTION TO DETECTIVE SUPERINTENDENT.

Following the very unusual Lloyds Bank job, I continued my work on the Flying Squad with maximum effort. I had successes in robbery investigations, and in September 1967, I was promoted to Detective Chief Inspector, and posted to West End Central Police Station, where I had started out as a Police Constable a few years earlier, in 1946. This was an area I had also worked whilst on the Flying Squad, and I mentioned this to Arthur Butler my Detective Chief Superintendent. He was not interested, and said that my position was now in a supervisory capacity which did not require me going into the type of places that I had visited on the Squad.

Furthermore, it was my job to see that young Officers did not get themselves into trouble by associating with the people using clubs and doubtful public houses. Good sound advice maybe, but to know what is actually going on outside in the streets of the West End one has to move around a little and keep up contact with those who would offer to assist, and I had a number of useful informants in the area.

I felt quite satisfied in my guidance of the younger officers, but only received confirmation of their integrity through my informants. This was of vital importance because of the many temptations I knew to be open to them in this sin-ridden area. Such enquiries that came my way, I was able to execute in a manner that earned me considerable praise from my superiors.

Early in 1969, I was transferred from the West End of London to Southwark in south-east London. There "M" Division is a quite fascinating wedge of the Metropolitan Police District, stretching from Docklands down to Crystal Palace. Once again, I was the second in command of the Criminal Investigation Department of the Division, a move that suited me. During my Flying Squad days, I had built up many useful sources of information in the area, which I now intended to call upon.

It was not long before I found myself in charge of a murder investigation, following the shooting of a bookmaker's clerk in Rotherhithe, an investigation I carried out to the satisfaction of my superiors

Then, following the finding of the body of a young Indian woman in the Thames at Rotherhithe, I was again called on to carry out the investigation. I succeeded in this case also, and arrested those responsible for her murder. This was indeed a very busy and heart-warming part of my Police service, in fact I worked like a beaver until 1972 on all manner of investigations.

After an almost embarrassing accolade from my Divisional Commander, Charles Renshaw, I was promoted to Detective Superintendent. In addition to my successful investigations, I also set myself the task again of guiding the younger Aides to C.I.D. in their work. I put them together as a squad, and with the aid of informants was able to set them off on some quite interesting investigations, which they concluded to the satisfaction of everyone.

On the retirement of my good friend Commander

Charles Renshaw, Commander Bill Brown took over the Division, and I was able to continue a happy working relationship with him.

This went along well until Christmas 1973, when he sent for me. I went to his office expecting another assignment or direction. He was busily reading some papers that were before him. I stood in front of him and waited. Then he looked up and said to me, "What's the matter, John, have we upset you or something?" I was mystified and lost for words, then replied, "What's the trouble, Guvnor? I don't think anyone is upset."

His reply to that was, "You are going to the Flying Squad on Monday. What have you to say about that?" Needless to say, I was just plain delighted, and said so. I told him that I had greatly enjoyed my service at Southwark, and regarded it as an honour that I had been recalled to the Flying Squad. The Commander stood up and shook my hand, wishing me good luck in my new job at the Yard.

For me, the return to The Flying Squad that month was a very happy occasion. I received a most warm welcome home from Commander John Lock, who had sent for me on my arrival to tell me that he was putting me in charge of The Robbery Squad. I thereafter took charge of a most useful team of officers, the majority of whom I knew quite well.

Additionally, in June 1974, not long after my arrival, I inherited Maurice O'Mahoney, a robber who, unfortunately for him, was arrested (together with some of his associates) by Detective Inspector Bob Connors and his team for a robbery at Phoenix Way, Hounslow.

Whilst on remand in Brixton Prison, O'Mahoney's partners in crime decided that he was the weak link in their chain of defence, if they had any defence at all. He was seriously assaulted by his erstwhile comrades, and on his next appearance at Brentford Magistrates Court, stated that he was guilty of the robbery and wanted to speak to the Police.

The result was that I set up an office at Chiswick Police Station, and took over most of the first floor whilst O'Mahoney was accommodated in the station cells. He just could not stop talking, and the accuracy of his information was such that he remained with us until September 1974, giving astoundingly accurate information about various robberies. Our activities with this man were thereafter guided by the forces of the legal establishment to an extent that surprised us all.

Bertie Smalls was, to my limited knowledge, the first and last criminal in this country who gave information about his robbing activities in exchange for immunity from prosecution, by producing evidence against his partners in crime. Thereafter, no such promise was to be made to a criminal. Thus, there was no chance of my being able to offer such a 'carrot' to O'Mahoney.

The result was that we were obliged to inform him that although we wanted to know all about his criminal activities, and those of his partners in crime, he had to understand from the outset that in due course he would be charged with that offence himself. The fact that he had assisted us would come out in the evidence, and he could use that point himself if he wished. The ultimate result and length of sentence was a matter for the final judge alone, over whom we had no control whatsoever.

It must be acknowledged that although he was a criminal, O'Mahoney was no fool. He realised full well that the original robbery he was charged with could result in his receiving a long sentence commensurate with the offence. Also, that by the same standard, by giving evidence against his comrades, the length of the sentence he might have been entitled to could be reduced considerably by his actions.

My Chiswick office was kept very busy processing O'Mahoney's information - to such an extent that I was asked to attend the Conference Room at New Scotland Yard, and give a talk on my activities at Chiswick. Then, standing up in what seemed like a pulpit in this vast auditorium, I gave my talk and noted the very obvious interest of the gathering of more Senior Officers than I had ever seen at a siting before.

It was at this point that I put forward the suggestion that perhaps we had reached a situation when such people as O'Mahoney would be regarded as 'Supergrasses'. The mention of that word, which I had just dreamed up, did cause some of the watchers to murmur something to their neighbours. Then, as I continued with my talk, I wondered whether I had gone a little over the top with my mention of this new word. I need not have worried, however, for that word is now common parlance when such people come to light.

You will appreciate that this was a time when all of my thoughts were directed towards investigations in hand. Notwithstanding the fact that I was so completely engaged in my work, I still kept a weather eye on the activities of young Chris. It had soon become clear to me that he was not study-minded, and bearing in mind the agonies I had experienced with studying earlier in my service, I had to sympathise with him, and respect his attitude towards the job. After that Lombard Street bank job, I was constantly in touch with City of London C.I.D Officers. All enquiries I made of Chris proved that he was quite a dedicated officer, respected by all. He became a Class 1 Motor Cyclist and vehicle examiner, and represented his Force in motorcycle events in the U.K. and overseas.

Chris also earned himself a good name as a surveillance officer, when he decided to concentrate of a group of East London 'Van Draggers'. The van used by this team was known, and it was kept under observation over a period of time. It was noted that the driver would pick up the van, then drive to the addresses of three of his partners in crime and pick them up. The idea was to capture this team red-handed, but as experience had taught me, capturing such people red-handed might be the ideal result, but the difficulties surrounding such an observation are numerous.

Clearly this team were looking for a suitable delivery van to rob, and many watches were kept on them, without good result. Perseverance, however, has its reward. They were seen to be closely following a delivery van. Then, when it was forced to stop in heavy traffic, one member of the team was seen to leave their vehicle and place a heavy inverted spike under one of the rear wheels of the van. When the traffic moved on, the rear wheel was punctured. One member of the team immediately left the vehicle and took the driver off to telephone for assistance. Then as the remaining members of the team started to transfer the load from the broken down vehicle, they were all arrested, including the man who had kindly taken the driver to the telephone, whilst his mates emptied his van.

A very satisfactory result in a most unusual case, with four villains charged with theft.

CHAPTER 18
THE END OF AN ERA

Just before the conviction of O'Mahoney, the Judge, Sir Carl Arvold, the Recorder of London, addressing me, said: "I would like to commend you and the officers involved in this case. All too rarely do I feel obliged to offer commendation but in this case in particular it is most unusual to hear the accused thank the Police for the way he has been treated and dealt with and I would like to thank you for the excellent work done by you and your officers."

At that date in September 1974, with a vast amount of work still my responsibility, the enormity of the tasks before me hit home. I could never see me completing the work involved before my accepted retirement age of 55 in August 1975. Furthermore, the complications of what still had to be done were such that I could not see me being able to just hand the package over to another officer, and go away.

I went to my boss, Commander John Lock, with my problem. I pointed out that I could not possibly complete the work that had accumulated before my retirement. Then with a little trepidation, I pointed out that if I left the service in 1975, I would only be entitled to a 29-year pension. I wanted to complete the job I was doing and would like, after being in the service so long, to be able to complete a 30-year service period. To my relief and surprise, the Commander agreed to my suggestion, but pointed out that the decision was not his alone.

Shortly after that interview, I was directed to attend the Chief Medical Officer's consulting rooms. With my past experience of attending for a check-up, and my personal opinion of my own fitness, I felt in my bones that this would be a very short meeting indeed. I attended at 9.30am as directed, but did not leave his presence until 3.30 that afternoon. I had never had such a complete and thorough examination. The great man's final words were: "On your way, Mr Swain,. I cannot find anything wrong with you. You are surprisingly fit for your age." We shook hands, and I left with a spring in my step, for I was now sure in my mind that my requested extension of service would be granted.

I did manage to complete the 30-year period, and in that period took on two further 'Supergrasses', Billy Williams, and James Trusty. During that final period it was agreed that my 'Supergrasses' and other prisoners were, between them, charged with the following offences:

Robbery 26
Attempted Robbery 3
Conspiracy to Rob 33
Burglary 82
Theft of lorry loads 2
Miscellaneous Crimes 96

You will have noted the number of conspiracies to rob that are quoted. Our enquiries proved without doubt that these planned robberies would have been put into effect had the Chiswick enquiries not been carried out in depth. We closely interrogated many more than those charged, and seized a number of shotguns, some with their barrels sawn off and shortened. Also pistols and powerful airguns, together with a collection of numerous rounds of varying calibre ammunition, much with the assistance of the Metropolitan Police Underwater Search Unit.

I saw this work through, and thoroughly enjoyed my 'swan song'. I spent my last weeks tidying up my paperwork, and handing over my Robbery Squad to my faithful and trusty deputies, Chief Inspectors Mike McAdam and Dave Dixon.

Then the day came when I handed over my Warrant Card to my then Commander, Don Neesham, said goodbye to my staff, and left the Yard. I remember, as I approached the security officer on my way out of the building, wondering whether I had left anything personal behind in my office, and checking over the contents of my pockets. I knew only too well that once past that security point, I could not get back into the building without going through the normal rigmarole that any visitor would be subjected to. Me, an ordinary visitor! The thought slowed me down considerably. I certainly did not relish the thought of having to return and ask the receptionist to arrange for me to be escorted back to what only minutes beforehand had been my personal office.

Once in the street, I could not resist turning to look up at the building I had known so well. The realisation came to me that I was now plain John Swain, ordinary citizen and one of the many unemployed. But that was not going to be for long.

I had not entirely wasted my personal time during the past two years. I had looked into some of the jobs that had been put my way for retirement, but did not fancy having to drive into London every day through the traffic to get to a City or central London office by 9am. There had to be better jobs open to me. Then I had thought of going into business as a Private Investigator, but thought again because the only Private Investigators I had ever met were not the type of people I would normally want to get involved with. This was a subject about which I needed good, unbiased advice.

I decided to call upon the one man who I knew would come up with such assistance - Vic Gilbert, the Deputy Assistant Commissioner in charge of Special Branch. My interview with Mr Gilbert was most enlightening. His opinion of Private Investigators was far higher than I would ever have imagined. He pointed out that we are a proud and efficient Police Force, respected world wide, but we have our 'bad eggs'. Furthermore, when they are dealt with, the publicity gives us a bad name. The same applies to Private Investigators. He was convinced that I would enjoy the work, and even thought I could even enhance the reputation of that profession in the eyes of the Service. His suggestion then was, "You should spend some time during the last years of your service sounding out probable clients for the future." What an interesting interview.

I left the Yard on that occasion with my mind made up that on my retirement, unless someone made me an offer I could not refuse, I would look further into this Private Investigation business.

Shortly after that meeting, I had occasion to call on Jock Wilson, the Assistant Commissioner of Crime, in connection with Robbery Squad business. I told him that I was contemplating going into business as a Private Investigator. He grinned and said, "Please John do not just call yourself a Private Investigator. You must put yourself forward as a 'Private Investigator and Security Consultant'. That gives you room to manoeuvre and the would-be client something to think about. First of all, however, go and see a good friend of mine, Lee Tracey, better known as just plain 'Lee.' Have a good long talk with him. He is a man who can give you more ideas than anyone. Furthermore, his advice will be the best possible that few can manage put together, and if you follow his guidance, you will succeed."

You will therefore appreciate that as I quietly made my way home that night in late August 1976, when I left the Yard for the last time, I felt happy in the thought that I had fair ideas about my future activity. Despite my confidence that I had made the necessary arrangements for my first big interview with this man Lee, I was still in something of a daze that evening. I had handed in my beloved Warrant Card, and would never be permitted to enter Scotland Yard again unless invited.

Having recovered from the shock (and I do not use the word lightly) of finding myself no longer a proud member of the Metropolitan Police, there was one thing I urgently needed. I even told Jock Wilson's friend Lee that I would be away for about a month This was because there was something I wanted more than anything else. Yes, a holiday. Away from it all, and certainly away from London. I wanted to get away as a private citizen, not as an off duty Police Officer, at the beck and call of a telephone. Not having to notify my whereabouts to my superiors in case a big job should break. In short, with no likelihood of being called out of my warm bed in the middle of the night to attend the scene of a murder, robbery or other serious incident. I wanted complete relaxation and peace of mind wherever I was.

I had no doubts about where to go, or what I was going to do. I went off to Scotland for a spot of Salmon fishing. Peter Anderson, probably one of the finest fly fishers in the world, was an old friend of mine. I telephoned him and told him of my intentions and sought his advice as to the best area to go to. His advice was more in line with an open invitation. He had a week free and therefore invited me to stay with him at his home in Kirkintilloch, just outside Glasgow. From there we could have a few days on the River Tay, and other spots near to where he lived.

I was made most welcome by the Anderson family, and spent a very relaxed and enjoyable week with them, and we are still in regular contact. I thus returned home refreshed, and with three weeks ahead of me in which to change my mode of life and settle down. I would no longer be troubled by the ringing of the telephone, for from then onwards telephone calls were all from friends, relatives or clients. Additionally, I was able to spend a little more time in my garden, my workshop, and giving my car that little extra attention it had never had before. In my heart I knew that I was going to enjoy myself very much from then on.

Following my introduction to Lee, I found myself very much drawn towards one side of Private Investigation that I knew nothing about, at least nothing further than the odd prosecution I had read about in newspapers and elsewhere, on the subject of Electronic Eavesdropping, Bugging, and Telephone Tapping. Now I had no intention of getting involved in the eavesdropping side of the business, but the countermeasures truly interested me.

With regards to my new friend Lee, he welcomed my enquiry and encouraged my interest in becoming a Private Investigator. To use his words, he felt that it was high time a senior C.I.D. officer from the Yard got involved in the private sector of investigations on retirement. According to him, so many like myself harnessed themselves to one of the larger companies who only wanted a name to quote as being in charge of security, primarily in order to satisfy their insurers that they were taking positive steps in relation to their company's security matters. He also pointed out to me that so many big businesses just ignored the probability of being 'bugged'. That, in their minds, was something that the Americans seem to love to talk about, and film producers seize upon to introduce as a point of unusual interest

The general attitude at the top was that if there was a leakage of company secrets, it was bound to be the result of the activities of a member of their staff who had received an offer or bribe from a competitor. This was an entirely new angle in the field of security for me. It was also something I wanted to get involved in. I expressed my great interest in the matter, and Lee told me: "Bugs are not on the open market in this country, but the next best thing is readily available if you shop around. They are used on stage by singers and comedians. A small battery fed microphone that clips on to a dress or suit is capable of being used in certain circumstances as a 'bug'. The transmission distance is small, and the battery power is generally limited. It does, however, present the idea as to what to do next." He stopped at this point, and said, "This is where I come in with my Scanlock."

He produced a fountain pen, scrawled his signature on a piece of paper in order to prove that it was, upon normal inspection, a quite ordinary working pen. The next move gained my even closer inspection. We went to an adjoining office where he switched on a small portable radio to a normal verbal broadcast. He placed the pen beside the radio, and we returned to the first office. He then produced his prototype Scanlock and switched it on. Almost immediately I heard the voice of the speaker we had just turned on in the other office. Then, to prove a point, he left me and returned to where he had left the pen. I could hear him clapping his hands as the almost deafening sound came over on Scanlock.

I then received a quick course of instruction on the finer points of this most interesting piece of electronic hardware. By tuning into the normal broadcasting channels, all came over loudly and clearly in addition some Police transmissions and local minicab chat came over similarly clearly. He then attached a hand held antennae, and switched over to a search mode, where all I could hear was a run of short regular clicks. He hung the strap of the machine over his shoulder and together we walked towards the office where the fountain pen had been left. The noise of the ticks became louder, and higher in tone.

At this point, Lee stopped to inform me that as we were obviously getting nearer to the 'bug' he would demodulate the machine – turn down the strength of his search. All was now quiet, and we walked into the office. I saw the radio on the desk where it had been before, but the pen was missing. "This is where you will appreciate the efficiency of the machine," he said, and with that he hung the Scanlock over my shoulder and handed me the antennae. He told me that he had hidden the pen, but if I swept round the room with the antennae, and moved in a grid pattern I would soon hear the high pitched ticks again.

Sure enough, I soon picked up the sound once more.

Then by demodulating, or turning down the search strength, I gradually eliminated each area until I almost touched the pen with the antennae. This was a most fascinating demonstration and personal action on my part, and something I was determined to get involved in. After the first shock of the price of the item, I assured my mentor that I would purchase one of his first models as soon as they were on the market. Also that I would need 'something' to practise with.

Having received a wonderful demonstration, I then received some words of warning. I was told that once I was satisfied I could use the equipment efficiently, I should let it be known amongst my clients and other interested parties that I was capable of carrying out electronic sweeps, and quote my rate for that sweep. I should always get a responsible senior member of staff to accompany me on such sweeps, firstly to ensure that all target areas of the company were covered, and to cover myself just in case any company equipment, such as a desk or cupboard, had to be moved during the search.

Thus it was that very shortly after this meeting, I purchased one of the first Scanlocks, together with a small gadget that clipped on to a nine-volt battery and emitted a pulse sound that could not normally be heard, but was picked up easily by Scanlock. Thereafter, 'Hunt the thimble' or rather 'Hunt the bug' became a regular activity at home with the very able assistance of my wife. She found all manner of strange places to hide this small accessory, but my machine never let me down, and all were found.

Since those far off days, I have carried out electronic sweeps all over of the UK and in many countries around the world. I have found bugs, but not very many. At the same time none of my clients have to my or their knowledge ever been bugged to date, and that for the most part has been because I always encourage clients to have their premises swept at regular but unscheduled intervals

From the very commencement of my activities as a Private Investigator and Security Consultant, I have had one very firm resolution. Apart from my confirmed belief in the efficiency of my Scanlock, I never discuss or mention the name of any of my clients to anyone. During the course of the following pages, while the reader may believe they 'know' the person or company I refer to as a 'client', they will get no confirmation from me.

My conversations and instructions from Lee put me into a serious study frame of mind. My army experience had served me well handling electrical circuitry. Actual electronics, however, was a different matter that I knew little about. I now had to spend time reading up and studying my Scanlock, a most interesting piece of equipment that I intended fully acquainting myself with before I ventured into the business world with it.

I did receive an offer from a brewery concern who wanted me to check up on the activity of bars in their hotels and public houses where the cash returns were not what they should be. After my initial discussions with them, I did carry out work for them for nearly a year. There was no doubt that I did manage to save them a lot of money. The trouble was that I was getting too well known in some of their problem houses. Additionally my business, thanks to the assistance of my good friend Lee, was expanding to the extent that I could see I would soon have difficulty in maintaining the success rate I had enjoyed to date. I mentioned this to the brewery official I was then reporting to, and he agreed to make other security arrangements.

CHAPTER 19
THE LEARNING ZONE

Lee had a manner of putting over his instructions that drew all my attention to his words. Explaining that there are so many ways in which the industrial spy can and will obtain confidential information, he mentioned some of the methods that could be used to gather audio information, and then dealt with the defence against such methods, finally giving me a complete run down on carrying out an actual sweep. He insisted that three important words must be in the forefront of my mind when carrying out such a sweep or search: DILIGENCE – VIGILANCE – INTELLIGENCE.

The obvious point to remember was that all devices used to 'eavesdrop' on a conversation require a microphone. That microphone might be surreptitiously introduced into the area in the form of a 'bug' or tape-recorder, or might already exist there in the form of a telephone handset. The microphone might be connected directly to an amplifier or tape-recorder, or built into a miniature audio transmitter or 'bug'.

Such transmitters can and may be manufactured as small as 1" x ½" x ½", hence they are very easy to conceal. They usually contain a microphone which collects the sound and transmits it by radio to a receiver that can be positioned from 100ft to three miles away. The more normal size of such a device is approximately 3" x 1" x

½" and as such they are ideal for a quick plant. For example, they can be fixed in such places as the underside of tables, chairs and desks, using double sided adhesive tape. They can be operated by battery or from a mains supply, but this takes longer to install. Don't forget, however, that all transmitters need antennae, a very necessary part of this equipment that on many occasions gives its position away.

Telephone transmitters are similar to those just mentioned, except that the microphone is replaced by a circuit which detects the speech in its electrical form by being physically connected to the telephone line. Such units draw in their power from the telephone line and hence will transmit indefinitely. They are usually concealed within the telephone instrument and transmit all conversation made to or from the telephone to which they are connected.

The Infinity Transmitter is a device again concealed. It may be inside the telephone instrument, or connected to the telephone line. This unit contains a microphone which picks up all conversation in the area around the telephone and relays these conversations to the caller. This unit is activated by the installer or his agent dialling the target telephone number and sounding a coded pitch or tone into the calling telephone's mouthpiece as he dials the last digit. The tone is heard by the Infinity Transmitter, which then prevents the telephone bell from ringing and connects the microphone to the telephone line. The conversations around the telephone line are then relayed over the telephone line to the caller.

With the expansion of Subscriber Trunk Dialling – S.T.D. – and International Trunk Dialling, the possibilities of this unit are both astounding and most worrying to the security man. Remember, the equipment can be installed in one country while the caller and listener can be in another country on the other side of the globe

Microphones which are super sensitive and contain an internal amplifier, are now no larger than 3/8" x 1/4" x 1/4". Such items can pick up conversation at ranges in excess of 25ft and as such are ideal for use in the transmitters mentioned. They can also be easily concealed in rooms wired out to a recorder or amplifier. The wires used may be specially installed for eavesdropping, or may even be spare telephone lines

The parts contained in the telephone hand set are a microphone and a receiver. All receivers or loudspeakers can act as microphones, and these can be connected to a spare telephone or intercom wiring which relay conversation to the transmitting unit or listening station. Additionally, the telephone may be 'bugged' or 'tapped' in a variety of ways:

(1) An indirect tap must be considered. It can be on the same principle as a telephone recording rubber sucker device, except that the induction coil may be placed in the proximity of the telephone line as well as the telephone instrument.

(2) Direct tap across the line at any point in the cabling network

(3) Spare wire tap, where a spare line is used to connect either a microphone, receiver or recorder, permanently to the cabling

(4) Certain modifications may be made to the circuit of the telephone which permit the use of the instrument for eavesdropping purposes as in the use of the Infinity Bug.

(5) The mains supply may be used to relay an electri-

cal signal from one area to another. Bearing in mind that a microphone converts sound waves into electrical signals, then by using a carrier transmitter connected to the mains a signal may be relayed from one room to another via the mains supply providing both plugs are used on the same electrical phase. The carrier transmitter can be built into the back of a socket outlet and work on a similar principal to that of certain intercom and burglar alarm systems.

(6) There are many other ways of gathering audio information, but the fact that the equipment required is costly and or bulky precludes its use for most industrial espionage purposes.

Passing from the 'bug', it must be remembered that there are three main parts to the detection programme, but it should be pointed out that a fourth part does exist. The fourth part is that of prevention and, if properly executed, it will reduce the need for parts one to three. Prevention includes key control, personnel vetting, document security, access control, effective locks and containers etc., but that is not the point of this task.

The three main parts are:

(1) The radio sweep

(2) Telephone wire and mains check

(3) Physical search

This is where you must get into your head the importance of Diligence, Vigilance and Intelligence

This detection programme should take place at a time when any radio transmitters would be working, such as just prior to and during sensitive meetings. Initially the sweep should be around the exterior of the room under search, remembering that a room has not less than six sides. The sweep is then conducted inside the room with the handset of the existing telephone removed off the hook. This applies power to any telephone transmitter thereby permitting their detection. At this point the presence of a voice operating or VOX transmitter must be borne in mind. Say something, or clap your hands. If the transmitter switches on, your equipment will pick it up.

All signals received should be identified, analysed, and where necessary located. The method is dependent upon the equipment available, but any illegal signal that is detected and subsequently identified as that of an illegal transmitter should be generally located, using the sweep unit and finally located by physical search. A tape recording of any known sound or radio signal which could be normal to that room is a useful aid to identifying an illegal signal.

(b) All telephone and intercom wires can be checked to ascertain whether there has been any illegal attachment made. All disused wires should be checked. A visual check of all communication units in the area and all cables that feed these units in the building should be made to locate any infinity transmitters, induction taps etc.

(c) The physical search must be methodical and thorough. Divide the room into quarters and work from the outside to the inside of each quarter. Move all furniture, and examine for any wires or signs that parts of the furniture have been moved. Tap all solid surfaces for hollow sections, look behind such items as pictures and pelmets. Remove all drawers and tables to check the area at the back of each drawer. Don't forget the bottom drawer! Below the bottom drawer there is space that an intruder could use to his advantage if such a place were not properly checked.

Check all heating and ventilation ducts, also areas of glass for contact or vibration microphones. Physically examine all electrical fittings, and junction boxes. Examine all surfaces and areas not normally visible. Never be content with a having found one item of eavesdropping equipment. A good operator will install more than one device, each one being harder to find than the previous one.

Where possible, carry out a second radio sweep during a sensitive conference or meeting to the outside of the meeting room or boardroom to check for any illegal transmitters that have been taken into the area by a person participating in that meeting. It is essential to control access of persons and furniture to any area that has to be checked and declared clear. There is no security in having carried out a detection programme, then allowing additional chairs etc. to be moved into the area or permitting unaccompanied access by cleaning personnel etc. An industrial spy will use sophisticated means to achieve his purposes – make sure that your defence capability is equally sophisticated.

One point remains that has not been mentioned, but is worthy of positive consideration in certain circumstances. The major call for sweeps is before sensitive meetings of the Board of Directors when the operation is carried out in the normal way. There are times, however, when the company Security Director will inform you that a well known outsider has been invited to visit and be present during the meeting in the Boardroom. Unusual as this may be, it does happen.

I have in such circumstances sat at a table outside the boardroom, close to the entrance door. There, with my equipment on the floor beside me switched on and wearing a small earphone, I have watched the Board and newcomer go into the Boardroom . I have never found anything this way, but it has always been appreciated by the Chairman and Company Security man. They would be aware of the reason for my presence, and no doubt have joined me in my firm belief that prevention is better than cure. On top of that, I have been satisfied in my own mind that had anyone entered that room with a miniature radio transmitter, my equipment would have located it immediately. Confidence in the equipment you use is so important.

CHAPTER 20
SOUNDING OUT THE FIELD.

Having thoroughly digested my mentor's words of wisdom, and satisfied myself that my newly purchased equipment was efficient, I sat back to work out a plan of action. I let it be known in the field of Private Investigators and Security Officers that I was capable of carrying out electronic sweeps, and quoted my rate for such sweeps. I cannot say I was very pleased with the somewhat cool reception I received. Finally, when speaking with certain colleagues engaged in security, one character informed me that he always found a 'bug' when he did a sweep.

Such a cool 'know-it-all' attitude I could not trust. He brought back to me one of the early warnings of my friend Lee, who had warned me of such boastful talk, and advised me never to enter into discussion with such people. He insisted that 'bugs' are rarely found. The object of the exercise was to ensure that those who might think it an easy matter to carry out eavesdropping on a particular client were made aware that his security was tight. Furthermore, that active measures are taken to preclude such illegal operations, and discover the eavesdropper.

Shortly after that meeting, I was most surprised to received a telephone call from the Chief of Security of a well known organisation, asking me to carry out a security sweep for them. I attended the offices and, under the watchful eye of the Office Manager who was to accompany me, assembled my equipment. I worked the first office in a grid pattern but although I spent quite a while there, found nothing of interest. My escorting Manager, however, seemed disinterested in the proceeding, and this troubled me a little. I felt that if the company had taken the trouble to call me in, they must have good reason.

I swept two other offices with a similar result. We then moved over to the large Boardroom. I immediately heard the familiar clicking indicating that there at least must be something of interest here. Demodulating my equipment, this had to be investigated. I worked the Boardroom in a grid pattern, and was led by further demodulation to the telephone on the Boardroom table. Closer examination of the telephone housing revealed a small transmitter quite expertly placed in it, using the power of the telephone line to power the 'bug.'

My escort looked pleased, and I felt extremely satisfied myself. I switched on my equipment once more preparatory to leaving, and moved towards the door. I was shocked. More clicks! Then, as I got nearer to the door, the clicks became louder. Surely not another 'bug', or was this what they refer to as 'standing waves'?

I demodulated the power once more and fine tuned the equipment right down. By this method I was led to a very small hole in the panelled door, behind which there must be a transmitter. Laying aside my equipment, I took a chair from the Boardroom table, stood on it and closely inspected the panelled door. There was a narrow strip of wood along the top of the door, which I could see had recently been moved. Then with my screwdriver, I prised up this strip of wood and removed it. In the centre of the door immediately above the position of the small hole mentioned was a larger hole about an inch-and-a-half across. Beside it was an ordinary drawing pin which secured a piece of thin copper wire, no doubt an antenna. I carefully prised up the drawing pin with my screwdriver, and drew a 'bug' up through the hole.

Precise measurement proved that the 'bug' had been lowered through the hole in the top of the door so that the microphone of the 'bug' was immediately opposite the tiny hole that had been pierced in the door by a small brad, about the size of a dart. Somebody had gone to a lot of trouble to put this gadget in place, but in my mind I had a strange feeling that I had been 'set up'.

There was no hysteria from the accompanying manager, who showed no particular interest or pleasure in the find. His only remark was an almost sulky "I suppose that's it then?" I was more convinced than ever that this was a put-up job. I had quoted my fee before taking on this job, however, and was determined to see it through, and ensure that I received my payment.

I told my escort that I had not finished my sweep of the areas indicated when I first arrived, and went with him to the remaining office. My equipment answered up almost as soon as we entered the room. The same clicking! This time I was guided to the ventilation grill in the wall. There, having removed the grill, I found a third 'bug'.

The attitude of my escort had changed considerably now. He then announced in a firm voice that none of his people believed that I would ever find the 'bugs'. He continued by stating that everyone had heard about the equipment used, but believed it all to be sales talk.

Clearly, beneath all of this, my guide was highly delighted with my efforts. We shook hands and he promised that he would tell certain of his friends about my effort and the equipment used. He also assured me that my account would be settled within a few days. It was!

This was the first true sweep that I carried out after taking delivery of my new toy, and practising with it at home, and I was simply over the moon with it's proven efficiency. Within a few days I was receiving calls from people I had never heard of, or been in touch with, asking me to carry out sweeps for them I also paid a call on my mentor, Lee, to give him an account of this rather unusual happening. His answer was very much in line with his previous instructions.

(1) He had made Scanlock, and knew it to be highly efficient, or else he would never have put it on the open market.

(2) Do not expect to find a bug every time you carry out a sweep. Remember, the client wants an answer to one of two questions, that is why he sent for you. He either wants you to tell him his premises are clear, or you find a bug.

(3) If you find a bug, the client is still worried about his own internal security procedures, which have permitted such an implement to have been installed in his premises without his knowledge

(4) When you announce that his premises are clear, you will also note his relief. Then remember what I have told you about 'loud mouths' who allegedly always find a bug. Just stop for a moment now and ask yourself what would have been the result if you had 'found' a bug on that recent sweep!

Life is undoubtedly very much a Learning Zone as time passes by. No matter what task you take on, you must be prepared to learn again and add to whatever little knowledge you have. This was an entirely new experience for me, and it brought home to me in a most positive manner the fact that dishonesty exists amongst those who project themselves to be genuine and above reproach.

Business for me improved from month to month, and I was called upon on a number of occasions to travel abroad with my equipment. Over the years that followed, I was required to visit countries that I had never previously been to. This was generally for British or American companies to check over their boardrooms prior to important meetings and discussions on matters of the utmost importance, and to advise such people on security matters and the dangers of counter-surveillance by competitors.

Rarely did I find anything during those sweeps, the reason being that I had educated such organisation on their security procedures. Thus they generally had their in-house security people check the important rooms physically before these meetings. I would then sweep the rooms immediately before the projected meeting, just in case there was a rogue within the staff of the establishment where the meeting was to be held.

On one occasion whilst in India, I did find one strange incident. I had always advised either my client or the security chief of any of the people I worked for against having a telephone in the boardroom or any room used for sensitive meetings. Most of them took heed of my advice, and if a telephone was connected within such an area, they would ensure that it was disconnected during the important or vital period. I felt proud of the fact that I had induced a certain in-house security awareness amongst many of my clients. As is always the case, however, some disregarded my suggestions. Thus it was that on one occasion in Delhi, I came across the menace that I had warned others about, but had not previously discovered during a sweep.

This sweep was in the offices of a large international company, and as soon as I entered the boardroom, my equipment gave me a warning. I was drawn towards the telephone on the desk of whoever would be in charge of the forthcoming meeting. This was one of the modern 'handy' telephones that can be lifted from its housing and handed to anyone in the room as they move around at will. All very nice and convenient - providing, of course, that security is what it should be, efficient. The trouble in this instance was that this telephone had been propped up and connected to an outside number. Thus, at the time that my equipment picked it up as I entered the room, it was transmitting audio and all other noises from the room down the line. Therefore anyone at the other end of the line would hear everything said in the room, that is, up to the time when use of the telephone was required.

My activities here caused quite a stir. As soon as I picked up the telephone, all I heard was the dialling tone. Whoever was at the other end of the line had heard our conversation prior to my picking up the receiver, and put their receiver down at their end.

The Office Manager who had accompanied me on this sweep was flabbergasted. The next step was to go to the company telephone exchange to find out who had asked for a line to the boardroom. The operator said she had no idea. Furthermore, as it was connected to the boardroom, she did not ask questions of those on the line because she thought whoever it was must have been someone of importance.

Whoever was the switchboard operator at the time

the connection was made must have had a hand in this action. Try as I would, however, I could not get anywhere with the operator, who seemed to have all of the necessary answers. She could not account for the connection, and was taken away for a grilling by the Office Manager. He too could get nowhere with her. However, in view of the fact that she insisted she had not left the exchange that morning, and the connection must have been made by her, he discharged her.

There was little doubt but that the operator knew who had made the original call or connection to the boardroom. Unfortunately, we had no evidence or indication as to who the listener at the other end of the line was. Suffice it to say, the company had had a severe shock. I stressed once again the stupidity of having such a telephone in a boardroom. The Chief Executive of the company, however, insisted that there would still be need for a telephone in the boardroom. His only concession being that the telephone would be disconnected from the wall plug whilst a meeting was in progress, and only connected through the company switchboard by a Board Member when needed. Additionally, that Board Member was required to leave his name with the switchboard operator when he requested the line to be connected. The operator in turn would then record the date and time of the request, together with the Board Members' names, in an official log, to be inspected by the Chief Executive or his deputy daily.

Furthermore, the boardroom was to be kept locked at all times when not in use. Also, the entry of cleaners or others using the boardroom for meetings was to be supervised, and noted in the record book on every occasion.

I am glad to say that although I am still in touch with that client, the system I instituted those years ago is still kept up, and there has been no further calls for my assistance there. Lessons are to be learned all the time in security, which is why it is such an interesting and challenging study. Finally, I would say that I am still in touch with my mentor Lee, who is ever ready to put me right when a problem arises.

CHAPTER 21
ANOTHER SWAIN JOINS THE MET.

By 1995, I had attained the respected reputation of being successful in my work of countering industrial espionage. My clients were many and various, but mostly of British or American origin, companies with international branches or connections.

The final result of my success in India, mentioned earlier, became well known in that country. Although it had only related to discovering that a telephone in a boardroom had been left virtually off-hook and connected to an outside number, it had caused quite a stir amongst Indian Security companies. I became quite heavily involved in discussions on that discovery, with my continued insistence that telephones in boardrooms were a constant danger and should be discouraged.

I was quite amazed how the story of that discovery had travelled around. At the same time, however, I was also very proud of the fact that the name of the particular company that I had visited was not known or mentioned. Then I received my reward! I was invited by Suresh SHUKLA, the Managing Director of SCI International Ltd., a large security organisation in the Gujurat City of Baroda, to travel to that city and give a talk on my security activities.

This outlining my work of electronic countermeasures, and demonstrating the same with my equipment. I attended as requested, and gave my talk to an assembly of Indian Security officers, including many senior Police and Army Officers. My talk went down well, and the bonus was that SCI international paid for the return fare to Baroda and the first-class hotel accommodation for myself and my wife whilst there.

On returning home from one of my many annual Salmon fishing trips to The Findhorn in Scotland, in late September 1995, I was both surprised and highly delighted to learn that my granddaughter Samantha, my son Christopher's daughter, had decided to join the Metropolitan Police on the 11th of that month. Furthermore, that she was on her initial Training Course at Hendon Training School. Samantha was my first granddaughter, the one I had named 'Boogaloo' in 1968 after the first words she had attempted to say to me, with just the glint of a smile, when I first saw her as a baby, then a new member of the Swain family. One of the treasures of my memory. How well I remember that very first day, a day I will never forget.

Never an idler, Sam, as she grew to be called, decided to learn hairdressing, an occupation probably influenced by her mother's known efficiency and occupation as a ladies' hairdresser.

Much took place during the following years, including the arrival of a second granddaughter, Natalie. Then in 1990, Samantha decided to travel to Australia, where she was joined the following year by her sister Natalie. In Australia, they both enjoyed the good life, a life so good that Samantha fell in love with and married a chef from New Zealand. Sadly, however, her husband was not a well man, and passed away in November of that year. Sam thereafter remained in New Zealand and Australia until 1994, when, as Mrs Corley, she decided to return to her homeland.

Samantha was not one to let grass grow under her feet. Once home, and in England, she met John Barber, and they decided to get married in 1995. It was not a happy union, however, and only lasted until 1997, resulting in divorce.

One of my proudest moments was during the afternoon of 29th January 1996, when I was privileged to visit the Hendon Training School, and witness the Recruits' Passing Out Parade. I was there to see Samantha, who had been awarded the Endeavour Shield, as the officer who had shown an outstanding level of commitment and effort in every aspect of the course. Pride stemmed from the thought that I had joined the Met in 1946, whilst on demob leave from the Army, as a First Class Warrant Officer. There, at Hendon, despite the amount of Army Law and regulations I had assimilated during my short wartime service, I had found that just passing out in a manner satisfactory to myself was exceedingly difficult

Yet this young lady, with little or no experience of law and regulations, passed out with absolute flying colours. Oh how I wished on that most memorable day, and since, that she had been Woman Police Constable Samantha Swain, not Corley.

On completion of the course, Woman Police Constable 514AB Samantha Corley was posted to Belgravia Police Station., where she became a very active member of the Grosvenor Sector group. There, whilst completing her two year probationary period, she again proved her metal, and passed with flying colours.

Thereafter, and truly accepting that I am an old 'has been', with no intention of intruding on Sam's private life, I kept myself informed on a very personal 'need-to-know' basis of her activities. The information I received indicated, on all occasions, that she would take on any job put to her; furthermore, she would complete that job without having to tap the brains of her superiors or worry them for assistance. She is very much a Swain at heart. In fact, she seemed to adopt exactly the same attitude towards work generally that my beloved father and I had done successfully throughout our very varied Police and Army service.

Samantha became known for her genuine willingness to help others, a point that came out on a number of occasions, such as when she had passed through the Station Office and seen members of the public waiting to be dealt with, callers she was always willing to assist the Station Officer with, of her own volition. I was also informed that she was held in high esteem by her senior officers for the help she provided to other members of her team, especially when dealing with younger and less experienced Officers. She was known to display tact when giving advice and guidance to them, in a manner that did not offend or belittle the other Officers' efforts. Unfortunately, however, she seems to have been to some extent bugged by misfortune, which first came to light in her marriages, and is perhaps accountable.

CONCLUSION

I have, as you will appreciate, had a very successful, interesting and at times quite exciting life, during which I have managed to travel to many countries of the world. At the time of putting this biography together, however, I felt that I had arrived at the time to relax a little, and set out the story of my life in full. I came to this conclusion in a very relaxed state of mind, having just completed an unusual but very successful job in Italy, Naples to be exact. I was lying back in my seat in the first class cabin of my British Airways flight back to London Heathrow, thinking.

Yes thinking, deep in thought. Not about the job I had just completed, but about my future. At 77 year of age, perhaps I could be excused for thinking about retiring. Perhaps I might even take time to write my life story. I had, after all, worked since leaving school at 14 years old. And if I did not start off too well, as time marched on, I was successful in every line of work that I took on. I put this success down to the fine example set by my father, who brought me up firmly but fairly throughout life. He was truly a prince amongst men who treated me like a man even when a boy, treatment that guided me to the one urgent desire in life to follow in his footsteps and be successful myself.

In order to confirm to the reader that my life story is

interesting, and worth reading, I will relate in some detail a job that I completed in Naples. This as an example of my work as a Security Consultant, specialising in electronic countermeasures – 'Sweeps' – debugging premises for clients, over the last 23 years.

In relation to the work, however, I must remind the reader that the identity of the client is sacrosanct, and will not be disclosed by me.

I have had many trips to Italy, a country I always enjoy visiting. My first trip there was during the war, whilst serving in the British Army. It was in those days that I began to learn a lot about the Italian people; their ways; their food; and their language, which came easily to my ears. Since the war, however, I have been called upon on many occasions to return to that country in the course of my business.

This particular 'Italian job' was carried out on behalf of a British company with numerous international branches. My task was to sweep the boardroom prior to their Annual International Board Meeting, which this year was held in Naples. The meeting was to be held in one of the better hotels in that city, where the food and service were excellent.

The room used for the Board Meeting was in line with the style of meeting rooms for business companies, generally available in better class hotels. I had never previously met the Chairman, who I shall refer to, but later learned that the invitation to carry out the sweep had come about as the direct result of a recommendation he had received from one of my regular clients. As to the Chairman himself, he had a somewhat military bearing and from appearance would appear to be quite an abrasive individual. His worry was that important information was going to be discussed at this gathering, and he wanted to be assured that nobody was listening in on the proceedings.

His idea was to have the boardroom swept the night before the meeting. I was to retain the key to that room over-night, and to report to him the result the following morning before the meeting commenced.

I told him that this was not the manner in which I generally operate, and suggested that I should, in addition, sweep the room in the morning immediately before the meeting, and report to him just before the members entered the room. Furthermore, I wanted a responsible member of his senior staff to accompany me during the sweep. He was all for this latter suggestion, but still wanted the job done the night before the meeting.

I gave the meeting room and surrounding area a thorough examination, but found nothing of interest. My companion remarked, "I didn't think there was anything here anyway." What a peculiar remark! I put the key of the room in my pocket, and agreed to meet him at 8.30 the following morning just before the meeting started. His attitude and reply to my statement worried me. Don't ask me why, but I felt that something was very wrong here somewhere, despite the fact that the room was undoubtedly clear. After my companion had disappeared from view, I locked the room, pulled some hairs from my head, and stuck them across the door jamb to mark the room.

I did not sleep too well that night. The attitude of my companion on the sweep kept my mind strictly on my business, and my responsibility for ensuring that the Boardroom was 'clear' when in use.

I got up at seven the following morning, washed,

dressed, and with my equipment made my way to the boardroom. My markings had been disturbed. Then as soon as I switched on my equipment, I picked up a very positive trace that had not been evident the previous evening. A transmitter was operating in the room. By demodulating my equipment, I was soon led over to the chair that would be used by the chairman of the projected meeting. Under the boardroom table, I noticed a small white plastic box attached by a wood screw to the underside of the table. The box was similar to those used by telephone companies as junction boxes for a spare telephone line to be attached when needed.

I got down on my hands and knees and unscrewed the box. It was hiding a small transmitting bug, with a nine volt battery attached, and taped to the underside of the table, with the antennae similarly attached by tape. In the position that the box had been fitted to the table, the microphone of the transmitter had been placed immediately opposite a hole that had been purpose made in the box for a telephone wire to pass through.

I removed the bug and detached the battery, then switched my equipment on once again. Immediately, I was getting another trace of a second transmitter. This was coming from the actual seat that would be used by the meeting chairman. I said nothing, but got down on the floor beside the chair. The underside of the chair was covered with an extremely well fitting piece of plywood, held in position with small angled pins in a similar manner to those pins used to secure the back plate of a picture frame. I made no sound. I got up and said in quite a loud voice, for the benefit of whoever had installed the bug, and might be listening, "That's it then. Another waste of time."

I had no desire to remove the plywood plate under the chair; my equipment had told me enough. There was definitely a second bug or transmitter under the seat, in fact built into it. It was well concealed and I wanted the client to see for himself the trouble that the opposition were prepared to go to before the meeting commenced. I walked out of the room and shut the door as loudly as was possible behind me. I also took the liberty once again of marking the door in a similar fashion just in case anyone wanted to inspect what was left of their activities.

I immediately made for the Chairman's room. I knocked on the door a number of times before I received a very gruff reply from inside. The door was finally opened by the Chairman, and when I explained my reason for disturbing him, he looked round for a chair and sat down. He was clearly most relieved, but at a loss as to what to do next. Finally, he said that it was very tempting to leave the second bug in position, and to feed the opposition with a lot of rubbish, but that would take too much preparation.

The important thing for me, however, was that the Chairman should see for himself exactly what had taken place so far. I returned to the boardroom. My markings had not been disturbed, so I waited for the Chairman. On his arrival, we entered, and he was highly delighted when I showed him the bug under his chair. We removed it, and he placed both bugs in his briefcase. I remained outside the boardroom with my equipment switched on whilst all members entered. I then retired to the hotel restaurant for what I felt was a well deserved breakfast.

That night, I was invited to join the Chairman for a special evening on our own. He wanted to know more about my line of business and what had guided me towards the electronic side of matters. I told him as much as I felt was correct, also that I had been engaged in 'de-bugging' work for the past 20 years, and we had a very pleasant evening together. I found him to be a perfect gentleman, a born 'no nonsense' individual, and a pleasure to do business with.

He was clearly shocked when I had originally disturbed him to tell him the news. He had been the one who called me in, and subsequent findings proved that he was right to call me in. He was delighted with the work I carried out, and even suggested that my action had probably saved his company a six-figure sum, on a matter that he would personally deal with.

The biggest surprise came when he said that he would use my services whenever he felt the need arose, and in addition, he wanted me to sweep his London offices every three months. Furthermore, I would not need to make appointments, but just call at three monthly intervals and get on with the job of checking the offices of all of his senior executives, then submit the bill direct to him for payment.

My trip to Naples was the first job I carried out for this company. We had agreed my charges before I commenced, and I received my payment by return of post.

The surprises came, however, when I subsequently learned that almost immediately following that most interesting visit to Italy, there was a quite dramatic reduction in the executive staff of the company. Clearly, the results of that sweep were taken very seriously, and acted upon. Also, I am happy to say that I was still in regular contact with the client, until I decided in 1999 that it was time I retired completely.

My remaining interest was to put together the story of

the 'Police Family Swain'. My son Christopher had been doing a good job in the City of London Police as a Motor Cyclist and Surveillance expert. He had worked as a member of the Criminal Investigation Department on Fraud Squad work. Then, at the time of the IRA bombing of the Stock Exchange, he was posted on a temporary basis to New Scotland Yard to assist in anti-terrorist work. He remained in this work for the following 18 months.

Returning to the City of London Police, he worked on the Motor Cycle Wing until his retirement in 1997. He retired with an excellent character, and was satisfied that he had received a number of impressive commendations from his superiors for work during his service.

Christopher's love of angling and shooting guided him very much towards country matters. It was therefore no surprise to me when I learned that he intended moving from his home in Biggin Hill, Kent, down to Devon. He is now firmly established as a Paramedic Ambulance Driver in his home town of Dawlish in Devon, working hard and regularly, and also following his love of Angling and Shooting.

My remaining interest now was to watch over the advancement of young Samantha's career. Unfortunately, however, the family enthusiasm was brought to a sudden and disastrous end on 22nd Novemer 1998. Whilst Sam was travelling in a Police vehicle answering an emergency call, the car was side-swiped by a car leaving a side street. Samantha, sitting in the passenger seat, received horrific injuries, mostly to her legs and ankles - injuries so severe that she was told she may never walk again. But, being a proper Swain, her reply to that statement was, "I bloody well will." She is currently making use of all her time attempting to put the problem right.

Sam had achieved her ambition to enter the Police Service. Her injuries, however, were of such a nature that she never resumed active duty, and was medically discharged with an exemplary character and Service Record on 27th May, 2000.

I was gravely shocked at this news, and knew in my heart that Sam was near heartbroken at not being able to continue in the service she loved. She just enjoyed doing good in the job, and wanted to keep up the family tradition in the Police Service. She genuinely felt that some of the rules and regulations covering injuries on duty should perhaps be amended, so that her usefulness could be applied to work, not as a front line Police Officer, but one of equal importance collating information on matters within her division. Thus she would be in a position to set the wheels in motion to ensure that the next unsuspecting criminal who came into her view was arrested by her colleagues.